# cupcakes
## ...made simple

This edition published in 2011
LOVE FOOD is an imprint of Parragon Books Ltd

Parragon
Queen Street House
4 Queen Street
Bath BA1 1HE, UK

ISBN: 978-1-4454-3055-3

Printed in China

Produced by Ivy Contract
Photography by Charlie Paul

## Notes for the Reader

This book uses imperial, metric, or US cup measurements. Follow the same units of measurement through-
out; do not mix imperial and metric. All spoon measurements are level: teaspoons are assumed to be 5 ml,
and tablespoons are assumed to be 15 ml. Unless otherwise stated, milk is assumed to be full fat, eggs and
individual vegetables are medium, and pepper is freshly ground black pepper.

The times given are an approximate guide only. Preparation times differ according to the techniques used by
different people and the cooking times may also vary from those given. Optional ingredients, variations or
serving suggestions have not been included in the calculations.

Recipes using raw or very lightly cooked eggs should be avoided by infants, the elderly, pregnant women,
convalescents, and anyone suffering from an illness. Pregnant and breastfeeding women are advised to avoid
eating peanuts and peanut products. Sufferers from nut allergies should be aware that some of the ready-
made ingredients used in the recipes in this book may contain nuts. Always check the packaging before use.
Vegetarians should be aware  that some of the ready-made ingredients used in the recipes in this book may
contain animal products. Always check the packaging before use.

# cupcakes

# introduction

Muffins, cupcakes, cookies, bars, and traybakes are without doubt the most versatile sweet treat you can make. While a large cake looks impressive, especially if it is beautifully decorated with frosting, it can really only be eaten from a plate, probably with a dessert fork. An individual cake, on the other hand, will travel, making it ideal for putting in a lunch bag, taking on a picnic, even just taken into the garden for a mid-morning or afternoon snack.

This really does not make an individual cake any less special, however, because—as you will discover when you start baking—these one-person treasures are packed full of the most sumptuous ingredients, from fresh or dried fruits to chocolate and nuts. We've even included an equally delicious "healthy options" section so that you won't miss out if you are keeping an eye on your intake of fats and sugar.

Of course, practicality isn't always the first consideration, and there are plenty of ideas for making sweet treats with more than a hint of indulgence! Frostings, decorations, and flavorings such as liqueurs turn a cake into a celebration, and we've included a section especially for those special occasions in life. The romantic at heart can chart a whole marriage in muffins, cupcakes, and cookies, from Valentine's day and the wedding day to the baby shower and the silver and golden wedding anniversaries, with all the birthday parties and other festive occasions along the way.

Baking is a great way to pass the time on a rainy day, and these recipes are ideal for children to help with—muffins and cupcakes need very little mixing, and take only minutes to cook. Children will love helping to decorate party cookies, fairy cakes, and cupcakes to celebrate Christmas, Easter, and Halloween—and they will certainly love to eat them, too!

# fruit & nut

# apple streusel cupcakes

## ingredients

### makes 14

½ tsp baking soda
10-oz/280-g jar tart applesauce
2 oz/60 g/4 tbsp butter, softened,
 or soft margarine
3 oz/85 g/scant ½ cup raw
 brown sugar
1 large egg, lightly beaten
6 oz/175 g/scant 1¼ cups
 self-rising white flour
½ tsp ground cinnamon
½ tsp freshly ground nutmeg

### topping

1¾ oz/50 g/generous ⅓ cup
 all-purpose flour
1¾ oz/50 g/¼ cup raw brown sugar
¼ tsp ground cinnamon
¼ tsp freshly grated nutmeg
2½ tbsp butter

## method

1 Put 14 paper baking cases in a muffin pan, or place
 14 double-layer paper cases on a cookie sheet.

2 First make the topping. Put the flour, sugar, cinnamon,
 and nutmeg in a bowl or in the bowl of a food
 processor. Cut the butter into small pieces, then either
 rub it in by hand or blend in the processor until the
 mixture resembles fine bread crumbs. Set aside while
 you make the cakes.

3 To make the cupcakes, add the baking soda to the jar
 of applesauce and stir until dissolved. Put the butter
 and sugar in a bowl and beat together until light and
 fluffy. Gradually beat in the egg. Sift in the flour,
 cinnamon, and nutmeg and, using a large metal spoon,
 fold into the mixture, alternating with the applesauce.

4 Spoon the batter into the paper cases. Sprinkle the
 topping over each cupcake to cover the tops and
 press down gently.

5 Bake the cupcakes in a preheated oven, 350°F/180°C,
 for 20 minutes, or until well risen and golden brown.
 Leave the cakes for 2–3 minutes before serving warm
 or transfer to a wire rack and let cool.

# carrot & orange cupcakes with mascarpone frosting

## ingredients

*makes 12*

4 oz/115 g/½ cup butter, softened, or soft margarine
4 oz/115 g/generous ½ cup firmly packed brown sugar
juice and finely grated rind of 1 small orange
2 large eggs, lightly beaten
6 oz/175 g carrots, grated
1 oz/25 g/¼ cup walnut pieces, coarsely chopped
4½ oz/125 g/scant 1 cup all-purpose flour
1 tsp ground pumpkin pie spice
1½ tsp baking powder

### frosting

10 oz/280 g/1¼ cups mascarpone cheese
4 tbsp confectioners' sugar
grated rind of 1 large orange

## method

1 Put 12 paper cases in a muffin pan, or place 12 double-layer paper cases on a cookie sheet.

2 Put the butter, sugar, and orange rind in a bowl and beat together until light and fluffy. Gradually add the eggs, beating well after each addition. Squeeze any excess liquid from the carrots and add to the mixture with the walnuts and orange juice. Stir into the mixture until well mixed. Sift in the flour, pumpkin pie spice, and baking powder and then, using a metal spoon, fold into the mixture. Spoon the batter into the paper cases.

3 Bake the cupcakes in a preheated oven, 350°F/180°C, for 25 minutes, or until well risen, firm to the touch, and golden brown. Transfer to a wire rack and let cool.

4 To make the frosting, put the mascarpone cheese, confectioners' sugar, and orange rind in a large bowl and beat together until well mixed.

5 When the cupcakes are cold, spread the frosting on top of each, swirling it with a round-bladed knife. Store the cupcakes in the refrigerator until ready to serve.

# shredded orange cupcakes

## ingredients

*makes 12*

3 oz/85 g/6 tbsp butter, softened,
    or soft margarine
3 oz/85 g/scant 1/2 cup
    superfine sugar
1 large egg, lightly beaten
3 oz/85 g/generous 1/2 cup
    self-rising white flour
1 oz/25 g/generous 1/4 cup
    ground almonds
grated rind and juice of
    1 small orange

### orange topping

1 orange
2 oz/55 g/generous 1/4 cup
    superfine sugar
1/2 oz/15 g/1/8 cup toasted slivered
    almonds

## method

1 Put 12 paper baking cases in a muffin pan, or place 12 double-layer paper cases on a cookie sheet.

2 Put the butter and sugar in a bowl and beat together until light and fluffy. Gradually beat in the egg. Add the flour, ground almonds, and orange rind and, using a large metal spoon, fold into the mixture. Fold in the orange juice. Spoon the batter into the paper cases.

3 Bake the cupcakes in a preheated oven, 350°F/180°C, for 20–25 minutes, or until well risen and golden brown.

4 Meanwhile, make the topping. Using a citrus zester, pare the rind from the orange, then squeeze the juice. Put the rind, juice, and sugar in a pan and heat gently, stirring, until the sugar has dissolved, then let simmer for 5 minutes.

5 When the cupcakes have cooked, prick them all over with a skewer. Spoon the warm syrup and rind over each cupcake, then sprinkle the slivered almonds on top. Transfer to a wire rack and let cool.

## variation

Replace the orange rind and juice with lemon rind and juice.

# cranberry cupcakes

## ingredients

*makes 14*

3 oz/85 g/5½ tbsp butter, softened,
   or soft margarine
3½ oz/100 g/½ cup superfine sugar
1 large egg
2 tbsp milk
3½ oz/100 g/¾ cup self-rising flour
1 tsp baking powder
2¾ oz/75 g/scant ¾ cup
   cranberries, frozen

## method

1 Put 14 paper baking cases in muffin pans, or place
   14 double-layer paper cases on cookie sheets.

2 Put the butter and sugar in a bowl and beat together
   until light and fluffy. Gradually beat in the egg, then stir
   in the milk. Sift in the flour and baking powder and,
   using a large metal spoon, fold them into the mixture.
   Gently fold in the frozen cranberries. Spoon the batter
   into the paper cases.

3 Bake the cupcakes in a preheated oven, 350°F/180°C,
   for 15–20 minutes, or until well risen and golden
   brown. Transfer to a wire rack and let cool.

# blueberry cupcakes

## ingredients

*makes 12*

4½ oz/130 g/generous ½ cup
    butter, softened
5 oz/140 g/¾ cup superfine sugar
2 eggs, lightly beaten
5 oz/140 g/1 cup all-purpose flour
½ tsp baking powder
4½ oz/130 g/¾ cup plumped
    dried blueberries
2 tbsp milk
confectioners' sugar, for dusting

## method

1 Put 12 paper baking cases in a muffin pan, or place 12 double-layer paper cases on a cookie sheet.

2 Place the butter and sugar in a large bowl and beat together until light and fluffy, then gradually beat in the eggs. Sift in the flour and baking powder and fold into the batter, then fold in the blueberries and milk. Spoon the batter into the paper cases.

3 Bake in a preheated oven, 350°F/180°C, for 25 minutes, or until golden brown and firm to the touch. Let the cupcakes cool in the pan for 10 minutes, then transfer to a wire rack to cool completely.

4 When the cupcakes are cold, dust with sifted confectioners' sugar.

# coconut cherry cupcakes

## ingredients

*makes 12*

4 oz/115 g/½ cup butter, softened,
    or soft margarine
4 oz/115 g/generous ½ cup
    superfine sugar
2 tbsp milk
2 eggs, lightly beaten
3 oz/85 g/generous ½ cup
    self-rising white flour
½ tsp baking powder
3 oz/85 g/⅔ cup dry
    unsweetened coconut
4 oz/115 g candied
    cherries, quartered
12 whole candied, maraschino,
    or fresh cherries, to decorate

### frosting

4 tbsp butter, softened
4 oz/115 g/1 cup confectioners'
    sugar
1 tbsp milk

## method

1 Put 12 paper baking cases in a muffin pan, or place 12 double-layer paper cases on a cookie sheet.

2 Put the butter and sugar in a bowl and beat together until light and fluffy. Stir in the milk. Gradually add the eggs, beating well after each addition. Sift in the flour and baking powder and fold them in with the coconut. Gently fold in most of the quartered cherries, then spoon the batter into the paper cases and sprinkle the remaining quartered cherries over the top.

3 Bake the cupcakes in a preheated oven, 350°F/180°C, for 20–25 minutes, or until well risen, golden brown, and firm to the touch. Transfer to a wire rack and let cool.

4 To make the buttercream frosting, put the butter in a bowl and beat until fluffy. Sift in the confectioners' sugar and beat together until well mixed, gradually beating in the milk.

5 To decorate the cupcakes, using a pastry bag fitted with a large star tip, pipe the frosting on top of each cupcake, then add a candied, maraschino, or fresh cherry to decorate.

# tropical pineapple cupcakes with citrus cream frosting

## ingredients

*makes 12*

2 slices of canned pineapple
  in natural juice
3 oz/85 g/6 tbsp butter, softened,
  or soft margarine
3 oz/85 g/scant ½ cup
  superfine sugar
1 large egg, lightly beaten
3 oz/85 g/generous ½ cup
  self-rising white flour
1 tbsp juice from the canned
  pineapple

### frosting

2 tbsp butter, softened
3½ oz/100 g/scant ½ cup soft
  cream cheese
grated rind of 1 lemon or lime
3½ oz/100 g/scant 1 cup
  confectioners' sugar
1 tsp lemon juice or lime juice

## method

1 Put 12 paper baking cases in a muffin pan, or place 12 double-layer paper cases on a cookie sheet.

2 Finely chop the pineapple slices. Put the butter and sugar in a bowl and beat together until light and fluffy. Gradually beat in the egg. Add the flour and, using a large metal spoon, fold into the mixture. Fold in the chopped pineapple and the pineapple juice. Spoon the batter into the paper cases.

3 Bake the cupcakes in a preheated oven, 350°F/180°C, for 20 minutes, or until well risen and golden brown. Transfer to a wire rack and let cool.

4 To make the frosting, put the butter and cream cheese in a large bowl and, using an electric hand whisk, beat together until smooth. Add the rind from the lemon or lime. Sift the confectioners' sugar into the mixture, then beat together until well mixed. Gradually beat in the juice from the lemon or lime, adding enough to form a spreading consistency.

5 When the cupcakes are cold, spread the frosting on top of each cake, or fill a pastry bag fitted with a large star tip and pipe the frosting on top. Store the cupcakes in the refrigerator until ready to serve.

# warm strawberry cupcakes baked in a teacup

## ingredients

*makes 6*

4 oz/115 g/½ cup butter, softened,
  plus extra for greasing
4 tbsp strawberry conserve
4 oz/115 g/generous ½ cup
  superfine sugar
2 eggs, lightly beaten
1 tsp vanilla extract
4 oz/115 g/generous ¾ cup
  self-rising white flour
1 lb/450 g small whole fresh
  strawberries
confectioners' sugar,
  for dusting

## method

*1* Grease 6 heavy, round teacups with butter. Spoon 2 teaspoons of the strawberry conserve in the bottom of each teacup.

*2* Put the butter and sugar in a bowl and beat together until light and fluffy. Gradually add the eggs, beating well after each addition, then add the vanilla extract. Sift in the flour and, using a large metal spoon, fold it into the mixture. Spoon the batter into the teacups.

*3* Stand the cups in a roasting pan, then pour in enough hot water to come one-third up the sides of the cups. Bake the cupcakes in a preheated oven, 350°F/180°C, for 40 minutes, or until well risen and golden brown, and a skewer, inserted in the center, comes out clean. If over-browning, cover the cupcakes with a sheet of foil. Leave the cupcakes to cool for 2–3 minutes, then carefully lift the cups from the pan and place them on saucers.

*4* Place a few of the whole strawberries on each cake, then dust them with a little sifted confectioners' sugar. Serve warm with the remaining strawberries.

# moist walnut cupcakes

## ingredients

### makes 12

3 oz/85 g/¾ cup walnuts
2 oz/60 g/4 tbsp butter, softened
3½ oz/100 g/½ cup superfine sugar
grated rind of ½ lemon
2½ oz/70 g/½ cup self-rising
    white flour
2 eggs
12 walnut halves, to decorate

### frosting

2 oz/60 g/4 tbsp butter, softened
3 oz/85 g/¾ cup confectioners'
    sugar
grated rind of ½ lemon
1 tsp lemon juice

## method

1 Put 12 paper baking cases in a muffin pan, or place 12 double-layer paper cases on a cookie sheet.

2 Put the walnuts in a food processor and, using a pulsating action, blend until finely ground, being careful not to overgrind, which will turn them to oil. Add the butter, cut into small pieces, along with the sugar, lemon rind, flour, and eggs, then blend until evenly mixed. Spoon the batter into the paper cases.

3 Bake the cupcakes in a preheated oven, 375°F/190°C, for 20 minutes, or until well risen and golden brown. Transfer to a wire rack and let cool.

4 To make the frosting, put the butter in a bowl and beat until fluffy. Sift in the confectioners' sugar, add the lemon rind and juice, and mix well together.

5 When the cupcakes are cold, spread the frosting on top of each cupcake and top with a walnut half to decorate.

# banana & pecan cupcakes

## ingredients

*makes 24*

8 oz/225 g/generous
    1½ cups all-purpose flour
1¼ tsp baking powder
¼ tsp baking soda
2 ripe bananas
8 tbsp butter, softened,
    or soft margarine
4 oz/115 g/generous ½ cup
    superfine sugar
½ tsp vanilla extract
2 eggs, lightly beaten
4 tbsp sour cream
2 oz/55 g/½ cup pecans, coarsely
    chopped

## topping

4 oz/115 g/½ cup butter, softened
4 oz/115 g/1 cup confectioners'
    sugar
1 oz/25 g/¼ cup pecans, minced

## method

1 Put 24 paper baking cases in muffin pans, or place 24 double-layer paper cases on cookie sheets.

2 Sift together the flour, baking powder, and baking soda. Peel the bananas, put them in a bowl, and mash with a fork.

3 Put the butter, sugar, and vanilla in a bowl and beat together until light and fluffy. Gradually add the eggs, beating well after each addition. Stir in the mashed bananas and sour cream. Using a metal spoon, fold in the sifted flour mixture and chopped nuts, then spoon the batter into the paper cases.

4 Bake the cupcakes in a preheated oven, 375°F/190°C, for 20 minutes, or until well risen and golden brown. Transfer to a wire rack and let cool.

5 To make the topping, beat the butter in a bowl until fluffy. Sift in the confectioners' sugar and mix together well. Spread the frosting on top of each cupcake and sprinkle with the minced pecans before serving.

# frosted peanut butter cupcakes

## ingredients

### makes 16

2 oz/60 g/4 tbsp butter, softened,
    or soft margarine
8 oz/225 g/scant 1¼ cups firmly
    packed brown sugar
4 oz/115 g/generous ⅓ cup
    crunchy peanut butter
2 eggs, lightly beaten
1 tsp vanilla extract
8 oz/225 g/generous
    1½ cups all-purpose flour
2 tsp baking powder
3½ fl oz/100 ml/generous
    ⅓ cup milk

### frosting

7 oz/200 g/scant 1 cup
    full-fat soft cream cheese
1 oz/30 g/2 tbsp butter, softened
8 oz/225 g/2 cups confectioners'
    sugar

## method

**1** Put 16 paper baking cases in muffin pans, or put 16 double-layer paper cases on cookie sheets.

**2** Put the butter, sugar, and peanut butter in a bowl and beat together for 1–2 minutes, or until well mixed. Gradually add the eggs, beating well after each addition, then add the vanilla extract. Sift in the flour and baking powder and then, using a metal spoon, fold them into the mixture, alternating with the milk. Spoon the batter into the paper cases.

**3** Bake the cupcakes in a preheated oven, 350°F/180°C, for 25 minutes, or until well risen and golden brown. Transfer to a wire rack and let cool.

**4** To make the frosting, put the cream cheese and butter in a large bowl and, using an electric hand whisk, beat together until smooth. Sift the confectioners' sugar into the mixture, then beat together until well mixed.

**5** When the cupcakes are cold, spread the frosting on top of each cupcake, swirling it with a round-bladed knife. Store the cupcakes in the refrigerator until ready to serve.

# peaches & cream cupcakes

## ingredients

*makes 12*

14 oz/400 g canned peach slices
   in fruit juice
4 oz/115 g/½ cup butter, softened
4 oz/115 g/generous ½ cup
   superfine sugar
2 eggs, lightly beaten
heaping ¾ cup self-rising flour
⅔ cup heavy cream

## method

1 Put 12 paper baking cases in a muffin pan, or place
   12 double-layer paper cases on a cookie sheet.

2 Drain the peaches, reserving the juice. Set aside
   12 small slices and finely chop the remaining slices.

3 Place the butter and sugar in a large bowl and beat
   together until light and fluffy. Gradually beat in the
   eggs. Sift in the flour and fold into the mixture. Fold
   in the chopped peaches and 1 tablespoon of the
   reserved juice. Spoon the batter into the paper cases.

4 Bake in a preheated oven, 350°F/180°C, for 25 minutes,
   or until golden brown. Let the cupcakes cool in the
   pan for 10 minutes, then transfer to a wire rack to
   cool completely.

5 When ready to decorate, place the cream in a bowl
   and whip until soft peaks form. Spread the cream on
   top of the cupcakes, using a knife to form the cream
   into peaks. Place the reserved peach slices on top
   to decorate. Store the cupcakes in the refrigerator until
   ready to serve.

# lemon & raspberry cupcakes

## ingredients

*makes 12*

4 oz/115 g/½ cup butter, softened
4 oz/115 g/generous ½ cup
    superfine sugar
2 eggs, lightly beaten
4 oz/115 g/generous ¾ cup
    self-rising flour
finely grated rind of 1 lemon
1 tbsp lemon curd
3½ oz/100 g/generous ¾ cup
    fresh raspberries

## topping

1 oz/30 g/2 tbsp butter
1 tbsp soft light brown sugar
1 tbsp ground almonds
1 tbsp all-purpose flour

## method

1 Put 12 paper baking cases in a muffin pan, or place
   12 double-layer paper cases on a cookie sheet.

2 To make the topping, place the butter in a saucepan
   and heat gently until melted. Pour into a bowl and add
   the sugar, ground almonds, and flour and stir together
   until combined.

3 To make the cupcakes, place the butter and sugar in a
   large bowl and beat together until light and fluffy, then
   gradually add the eggs. Sift in the flour and fold into
   the mixture. Fold in the lemon rind, lemon curd, and
   raspberries. Spoon the batter into the paper cases.
   Add the topping to cover the top of each cupcake and
   press down gently.

4 Bake in a preheated oven, 400°F/200°C, for 15–20
   minutes, or until golden brown and firm to the touch.
   Let the cupcakes cool for 10 minutes, then transfer to
   a wire rack to cool completely.

# fresh raspberry cupcakes

## ingredients

*makes 12*

9½ oz/275 g/2¼ cups fresh
    raspberries
5 fl oz/150 ml/⅔ cup sunflower oil
2 eggs
¾ cup superfine sugar
½ tsp vanilla extract
9½ oz/275 g/2 cups all-purpose
    flour
¾ tsp baking soda

## topping

5 fl oz/150 ml/⅔ cup heavy cream
12 fresh raspberries
small mint leaves, for decorating

## method

1 Put 12 paper baking cases in a muffin pan, or place 12 double-layer paper cases on a cookie sheet.

2 Place the raspberries in a large bowl and crush lightly with a fork.

3 Place the oil, eggs, sugar, and vanilla extract in a large bowl and whisk together until well combined. Sift in the flour and baking soda and fold into the batter, then fold in the crushed raspberries. Spoon the batter into the paper cases.

4 Bake in a preheated oven, 350°F/180°C, for 30 minutes, or until golden brown and firm to the touch. Let the cupcakes cool in the pan for 10 minutes, then transfer to a wire rack to cool completely.

5 When ready to decorate, place the cream in a bowl and whip until soft peaks form. Spread the cream on top of the cupcakes, using a knife to smooth the cream. Top each cupcake with a raspberry and decorate with mint leaves. Store the cupcakes in the refrigerator until ready to serve.

# tropical banana
# & passion fruit muffins

## ingredients

### makes 12

2 bananas
5 fl oz/150 ml/about ⅔ cup milk
10 oz/280 g/2 cups all-purpose
    flour
1 tbsp baking powder
pinch of salt
4 oz/115 g/generous ½ cup light
    brown sugar
2 eggs
6 tbsp sunflower oil or 6 tbsp
    butter, melted and cooled
1 tsp vanilla extract

### topping

2 passion fruits
2 tbsp honey

## method

1 Line a 12-cup muffin pan with 12 muffin liners. Mash
   the bananas and put in a pitcher. Add enough milk to
   make the puree up to a heaping 1 cup.

2 Sift together the flour, baking powder, and salt into a
   large bowl. Stir in the sugar.

3 Place the eggs in a large pitcher or bowl and beat
   lightly, then beat in the banana and milk mixture, oil,
   and vanilla extract. Make a well in the center of the dry
   ingredients and pour in the beaten liquid ingredients.
   Stir gently until just combined; do not overmix. Spoon
   the batter into the muffin liners.

4 Bake in a preheated oven, 400°F/200°C, for 20 minutes,
   or until well risen, golden brown, and firm to the touch.
   Let cool in the pan for 5 minutes, then transfer to a wire
   rack to cool completely.

5 Meanwhile, halve the passion fruits and spoon the
   pulp into a small saucepan. Add the honey and heat
   very gently until warmed through. Spoon on top of the
   muffins before serving.

# toffee apple cakes

## ingredients

*makes 12*

2 oz/60 g/4 tbsp butter, plus extra
  for greasing
2 apples
1 tbsp lemon juice
9 oz/250 g/1¾ cups all-purpose
  flour
2 tsp baking powder
1½ tsp ground cinnamon
2½ oz/70 g/⅓ cup light brown
  sugar
3½ fl oz/100 ml/generous
  ⅓ cup milk
3½ fl oz/100 ml/generous ⅓ cup
  apple juice
1 egg, lightly beaten

### topping
2 tbsp light cream
1½ oz/40 g/¼ cup light
  brown sugar
½ oz/15 g/1 tbsp butter

## method

*1* Grease a 12-cup muffin pan. Core and coarsely grate
one of the apples and set aside. Slice the remaining
apple into ¼ inch/5 mm thick wedges and toss in the
lemon juice. Sift together the flour, baking powder, and
cinnamon, then stir in the sugar and grated apple.

*2* Place the butter in a saucepan and heat gently until
melted, then mix with the milk, apple juice, and egg.
Stir the liquid mixture into the dry ingredients, mixing
lightly until just combined.

*3* Spoon the batter into the muffin pan and arrange
2 apple slices on top of each. Bake in a preheated oven,
400°F/200°C, for 20–25 minutes, or until risen, firm,
and golden brown. Run a knife around the edge of
each cake to loosen, then transfer to a wire rack to
cool completely.

*4* For the topping, place all the ingredients in a small pan
and heat, stirring, until the sugar is dissolved. Increase
the heat and boil for 2 minutes, or until syrupy. Cool
slightly, then drizzle over the cakes and let set.

# apple & cinnamon muffins

## ingredients

### makes 6

3 oz/85 g/scant ⅔ cup all-purpose
   whole wheat flour
2½ oz/70 g/½ cup all-purpose
   white flour
1½ tsp baking powder
pinch of salt
1 tsp ground cinnamon
1½ oz/40 g/scant ¼ cup golden
   superfine sugar
2 small eating apples, peeled,
   cored, and finely chopped
4 fl oz/125 ml/½ cup milk
1 egg, beaten
2 oz/60 g/4 tbsp butter, melted

## topping

12 brown sugar lumps,
   coarsely crushed
½ tsp ground cinnamon

## method

1 Line a muffin pan with 6 muffin liners.

2 Sift both flours, baking powder, salt, and cinnamon together into a large bowl and stir in the sugar and chopped apples. Place the milk, egg, and butter in a separate bowl and mix. Add the wet ingredients to the dry ingredients and gently stir until just combined.

3 Divide the batter evenly among the muffin liners. To make the topping, mix the crushed sugar lumps and cinnamon together and sprinkle over the muffins. Bake in a preheated oven, 400°F/200°C, for 20–25 minutes, or until risen and golden. Remove the muffins from the oven and serve warm or place them on a wire rack and let cool.

# fig & almond muffins

## ingredients

### makes 12

2 tbsp sunflower or peanut oil,
　plus extra for oiling (if using)
9 oz/250 g/generous
　1¾ cups all-purpose flour
1 tsp baking soda
½ tsp salt
8 oz/225 g/1 cup raw sugar
3 oz/85 g/generous ½ cup dried
　figs, chopped
4 oz/115 g/1 cup almonds,
　chopped
7 fl oz/200 ml/1 cup water
1 tsp almond extract
2 tbsp chopped almonds,
　to decorate

## method

1 Oil a 12-cup muffin pan with sunflower oil, or line it with 12 muffin liners.

2 Sift the flour, baking soda, and salt into a mixing bowl. Then add the raw sugar and stir together.

3 In a separate bowl, mix the figs, almonds, and remaining sunflower oil together. Then stir in the water and almond extract. Add the fruit and nut mixture to the flour mixture and gently stir together. Do not overstir—it is fine for it to be a little lumpy.

4 Divide the muffin batter evenly among the 12 cups in the muffin pan or the muffin liners (they should be about two-thirds full), then sprinkle over the remaining chopped almonds to decorate. Transfer to a preheated oven, 375°F/190°C, and bake for 25 minutes, or until risen and golden.

5 Remove the muffins from the oven and serve warm, or place them on a wire rack and let cool.

# cranberry & cheese muffins

## ingredients

*makes 18*

butter, for greasing
8 oz/225 g/generous
    1½ cups all-purpose flour
2 tsp baking powder
½ tsp salt
2 oz/55 g/¼ cup
    superfine sugar
2 oz/60 g/4 tbsp butter, melted
2 large eggs, lightly beaten
6 fl oz/175 ml/¾ cup milk
4 oz/115 g/generous 1 cup fresh
    cranberries
1 oz/25 g/¼ cup freshly grated
    Parmesan cheese

## method

*1* Lightly grease 2 x 9-cup muffin pans with butter.

*2* Sift the flour, baking powder, and salt into a mixing bowl. Stir in the superfine sugar.

*3* In a separate bowl, combine the butter, beaten eggs, and milk, then pour into the bowl of dry ingredients. Mix lightly together until all of the ingredients are evenly combined, then stir in the fresh cranberries.

*4* Divide the batter evenly among the prepared 18 cups in the muffin pans. Sprinkle the grated Parmesan cheese over the top. Transfer to a preheated oven, 400°F/200°C, and bake for 20 minutes, or until the muffins are well risen and a golden brown color.

*5* Remove the muffins from the oven and let them cool slightly in the pans. Place the muffins on a wire rack and let cool completely.

# nectarine & banana muffins

## ingredients

### serves 12

2½ fl oz/75 ml/generous ⅓ cup sunflower or peanut oil, plus extra for oiling (if using)
9 oz/250 g/generous 1¾ cups all-purpose flour
1 tsp baking soda
¼ tsp salt
¼ tsp allspice
3½ oz/100 g/½ cup superfine sugar
2 oz/55 g/½ cup shelled almonds, chopped
6 oz/175 g ripe nectarine, peeled and chopped
1 ripe banana, sliced
2 large eggs
3 fl oz/90 ml/⅓ cup thick strained plain or banana-flavored yogurt
1 tsp almond extract

## method

1 Oil a 12-cup muffin pan with sunflower oil, or line it with 12 muffin liners.

2 Sift the flour, baking soda, salt, and allspice into a mixing bowl. Then add the superfine sugar and chopped almonds and stir together.

3 In a separate large bowl, mash the nectarine and banana together, then stir in the eggs, remaining sunflower oil, yogurt, and almond extract. Add the mashed fruit mixture to the flour mixture and then gently stir together until just combined. Do not overstir the batter—it is fine for it to be a little lumpy.

4 Divide the muffin batter evenly among the 12 cups in the muffin pan or the muffin liners (they should be about two-thirds full). Transfer to a preheated oven, 400°F/200°C, and bake for 20 minutes, or until risen and golden. Serve warm from the oven, or place them on a wire rack and let cool.

# tropical coconut muffins

## ingredients

### makes 12

1 tbsp sunflower or peanut oil,
    for oiling (if using)
9 oz/250 g/generous
    1¾ cups all-purpose flour
1 tsp baking powder
1 tsp baking soda
½ tsp allspice
4 oz/115 g/½ cup butter
8 oz/225 g/1 cup packed
    brown sugar
2 large eggs, beaten
2 tbsp thick plain, banana, or
    pineapple-flavored yogurt
1 tbsp rum
1 ripe banana, sliced
2¾ oz/75 g canned pineapple
    rings, drained and chopped
⅜ cup dry unsweetened coconut

### topping

4 tbsp raw sugar
1 tsp allspice
1 oz/25 g/scant ¼ cup dry
    unsweetened coconut

## method

1 Oil a 12-cup muffin pan with sunflower oil, or line it with 12 muffin liners.

2 Sift the flour, baking powder, baking soda, and allspice into a mixing bowl.

3 In a separate large bowl, cream together the butter and brown sugar, then stir in the eggs, yogurt, and rum. Add the banana, pineapple, and dry unsweetened coconut and mix together gently. Add the pineapple mixture to the flour mixture and then gently stir together until just combined. Do not overstir the batter—it is fine for it to be a little lumpy.

4 Divide the muffin batter evenly among the 12 cups in the muffin pan or the muffin liners (they should be about two-thirds full). To make the topping, mix the raw sugar and allspice together and sprinkle over the muffins. Sprinkle over the dry unsweetened coconut, then transfer to a preheated oven, 400°F/200°C. Bake for 20 minutes, or until risen and golden. Remove the muffins from the oven and serve warm, or place them on a wire rack and let cool.

# apple shortcakes

## ingredients

*makes 4*

1 oz/30 g/2 tbsp butter, cut into
    small pieces, plus extra
    for greasing
5½ oz/150 g/generous 1 cup
    all-purpose flour, plus extra
    for dusting
½ tsp salt
1 tsp baking powder
1 tbsp superfine sugar
2 fl oz/50 ml/¼ cup milk
confectioners' sugar, for dusting

### filling

3 dessert apples, peeled, cored,
    and sliced
3½ oz/100 g/½ cup superfine sugar
1 tbsp lemon juice
1 tsp ground cinnamon
10 fl oz/300 ml/1¼ cups water
5 fl oz/150 ml/⅔ cup heavy cream,
    lightly whipped

## method

1 Lightly grease a cookie sheet. Sift the flour, salt, and baking powder into a large bowl. Stir in the sugar, then add the butter and rub it in with your fingertips until the mixture resembles fine bread crumbs. Pour in the milk and mix to a soft dough.

2 On a lightly floured counter, knead the dough lightly, then roll out to 1/2-inch/1-cm thick. Stamp out 4 circles, using a 2-inch/5-cm cutter. Transfer the circles to the prepared cookie sheet.

3 Bake in a preheated oven, 425°F/220°C, for 15 minutes, until the shortcakes are well risen and lightly browned. Let cool.

4 To make the filling, place the apple, sugar, lemon juice, and cinnamon in a pan. Add the water, bring to a boil and let simmer, uncovered, for 5–10 minutes, or until the apples are tender. Cool slightly, then remove the apples from the pan.

5 To serve, split the shortcakes in half. Place each bottom half on an individual serving plate and spoon on a fourth of the apple slices, then the cream. Place the other half of the shortcake on top. Serve dusted with confectioners' sugar.

# maple pecan tarts

## ingredients

*makes 12*

### dough

5 oz/150 g/1 cup all-purpose flour,
   plus extra for dusting
3 oz/85 g/6 tbsp butter
2 oz/55 g/¼ cup golden superfine
   sugar
2 egg yolks

### filling

2 tbsp maple syrup
5 fl oz/150 ml/⅔ cup heavy cream
4 oz/115 g/generous ½ cup golden
   superfine sugar
pinch of cream of tartar
6 tbsp water
6 oz/175 g/1 cup pecans
12 pecan nut halves, to decorate

## method

1 Sift the flour into a large bowl, then cut the butter into pieces and rub it into the flour using your fingertips until the mixture resembles bread crumbs. Stir in the sugar, then stir in the egg yolks to make a smooth dough. Wrap in plastic wrap and chill in the refrigerator for 30 minutes.

2 On a floured counter, roll out the pastry thinly, cut out circles, and use to line 12 tartlet pans. Prick the bottoms and press a piece of foil into each tart shell. Bake in a preheated oven, 400°F/200°C, for 10–15 minutes, or until light golden. Remove the foil and bake for a further 2–3 minutes. Let cool on a wire rack.

3 To make the filling, mix together half the maple syrup and half the cream in a bowl. Place the sugar, cream of tartar, and water in a pan over low heat and stir until the sugar dissolves. Bring to a boil and continue boiling until light golden. Remove from the heat and stir in the maple syrup and cream mixture.

4 Return to the heat and cook to the "soft ball" stage, when a little of the mixture forms a soft ball when dropped into cold water. Stir in the remaining cream and let stand until warm. Brush the syrup over the edges of the tarts. Place the pecans in the shells, spoon in the toffee and top with a nut half. Let cool.

# summer fruit tartlets

## ingredients

*makes 12*

### dough

7 oz/200 g/scant 1½ cups
    all-purpose flour, plus extra
    for dusting
3 oz/85 g/generous ¾ cup
    confectioners' sugar
2 oz/55 g/⅔ cup ground almonds
4 oz/115 g/½ cup butter
1 egg yolk
1 tbsp milk

### filling

8 oz/225 g/1 cup cream cheese
confectioners' sugar, to taste,
    plus extra for dusting
12 oz/350 g/2½ cups fresh
    summer fruits, such as red
    and white currants, blueberries,
    raspberries, and small
    strawberries

## method

1 To make the dough, sift the flour and confectioners' sugar into a bowl. Stir in the ground almonds. Add the butter and rub in until the mixture resembles bread crumbs. Add the egg yolk and milk and work in with a spatula, then mix with your fingers until the dough binds together. Wrap the dough in plastic wrap and let chill in the refrigerator for 30 minutes.

2 On a floured counter, roll out the dough and use to line 12 deep tartlet or individual brioche pans. Prick the bottoms. Press a piece of foil into each tartlet, covering the edges, and bake in a preheated oven, 400°F/200°C, for 10–15 minutes, or until light golden brown. Remove the foil and bake for an additional 2–3 minutes. Transfer to a wire rack to cool.

3 To make the filling, place the cream cheese and confectioners' sugar in a bowl and mix together. Place a spoonful of filling in each tart shell and arrange the fruit on top. Dust with sifted confectioners' sugar and serve.

# chocolate

# jumbo chocolate chip cupcakes

## ingredients

*makes 8*

3½ oz/100 g/7 tbsp soft margarine
3½ oz/100 g/½ cup superfine sugar
2 large eggs
3½ oz/100 g/scant ¾ cup
    self-rising white flour
3½ oz/100 g/generous ½ cup
    semisweet chocolate chips

## method

*1* Put 8 paper baking cases in a muffin pan, or place 8 double-layer paper cases on a cookie sheet.

*2* Put the margarine, sugar, eggs, and flour in a large bowl and, using an electric hand whisk, beat together until just smooth. Fold in the chocolate chips. Spoon the batter into the paper cases.

*3* Bake the cupcakes in a preheated oven, 375°F/190°C, for 20–25 minutes, or until well risen and golden brown. Transfer to a wire rack to cool.

## variation

Replace the semisweet chocolate chips with 2 oz/55 g sweet chocolate chips and 2 oz/55 g chopped hazelnuts.

# soft-centered chocolate cupcakes

## ingredients

*makes 8*

2 oz/60 g/4 tbsp soft margarine
2 oz/60 g/generous ¼ cup
    superfine sugar
1 large egg
3 oz/85 g/generous ½ cup
    self-rising flour
1 tbsp unsweetened cocoa
2 oz/55 g semisweet chocolate
confectioners' sugar, for dusting

## method

1 Put 8 paper baking cases in a muffin pan, or place 8 double-layer paper cases on a cookie sheet.

2 Put the margarine, sugar, egg, flour, and cocoa in a large bowl and, using an electric hand whisk, beat together until just smooth.

3 Spoon half of the batter into the paper cases. Using a teaspoon, make an indentation in the center of each cake. Break the chocolate evenly into 8 squares and place a piece in each indentation, then spoon the remaining cake batter on top.

4 Bake the cupcakes in a preheated oven, 375°F/190°C, for 20 minutes, or until well risen and springy to the touch. Leave the cupcakes for 2–3 minutes before serving warm, dusted with sifted confectioners' sugar.

# mocha cupcakes with whipped cream

## ingredients

### makes 20

2 tbsp instant espresso
    coffee powder
3 oz/85 g/6 tbsp butter
3 oz/85 g/scant ½ cup
    superfine sugar
1 tbsp honey
7 fl oz/200 ml/scant 1 cup water
8 oz/225 g/generous 1½ cups
    all-purpose flour
2 tbsp unsweetened cocoa
1 tsp baking soda
3 tbsp milk
1 large egg, lightly beaten

### topping

8 fl oz/225 ml/1 cup
    whipping cream
unsweetened cocoa, sifted,
    for dusting

## method

*1* Put 20 paper baking cases in muffin pans, or place 20 double-layer paper cases on cookie sheets.

*2* Put the coffee powder, butter, sugar, honey, and water in a pan and heat gently, stirring, until the sugar has dissolved. Bring to a boil, then reduce the heat and let simmer for 5 minutes. Pour into a large heatproof bowl and let cool.

*3* When the mixture has cooled, sift in the flour and cocoa. Dissolve the baking soda in the milk, then add to the mixture with the egg and beat together until smooth. Spoon the batter into the paper cases.

*4* Bake the cupcakes in a preheated oven, 350°F/180°C, for 15–20 minutes, or until well risen and firm to the touch. Transfer to a wire rack to cool.

*5* For the topping, whisk the cream in a bowl until it holds its shape. Just before serving, spoon heaped teaspoonfuls of cream on top of each cake, then dust lightly with sifted cocoa. Store the cupcakes in the refrigerator until ready to serve.

# devil's food cakes with chocolate frosting

## ingredients

### makes 18

1¾oz/50 g/3½ tbsp soft margarine
4 oz/115 g/generous ½ cup firmly
　　packed brown sugar
2 large eggs
4 oz/115 g/generous ¾ cup
　　all-purpose flour
½ tsp baking soda
1 oz/25 g/generous ¼ cup
　　unsweetened cocoa
4 fl oz/125 ml/½ cup sour cream

### frosting

4½ oz/125 g semisweet chocolate
2 tbsp superfine sugar
5 fl oz/150 ml/⅔ cup sour cream

### chocolate curls (optional)

3½ oz/100 g semisweet chocolate

## method

1 Put 18 paper baking cases in muffin pans, or place 18 double-layer paper cases on cookie sheets.

2 Put the margarine, sugar, eggs, flour, baking soda, and cocoa in a large bowl and, using an electric hand whisk, beat together until just smooth. Using a metal spoon, fold in the sour cream. Spoon the batter into the paper cases.

3 Bake the cupcakes in a preheated oven, 350°F/180°C, for 20 minutes, or until well risen and firm to the touch. Transfer to a wire rack to cool.

4 To make the frosting, break the chocolate into a heatproof bowl. Set the bowl over a pan of gently simmering water and heat until melted, stirring occasionally. Remove from the heat and let cool slightly, then whisk in the sugar and sour cream until combined. Spread the frosting over the tops of the cupcakes and let set in the refrigerator before serving. If liked, serve decorated with chocolate curls made by shaving semisweet chocolate with a potato peeler.

# tiny chocolate cupcakes with ganache frosting

## ingredients

*makes 20*

2 oz/60 g/4 tbsp butter, softened
2 oz/60 g/generous ¼ cup
    superfine sugar
1 large egg, lightly beaten
2 oz/55 g/scant ½ cup white
    self-rising flour
2 tbsp unsweetened cocoa
1 tbsp milk
20 chocolate-coated coffee beans,
    to decorate (optional)

## frosting

3½ oz/100 g semisweet chocolate
3½ fl oz/100 ml/generous
    ⅓ cup heavy cream

## method

*1* Place 20 mini paper baking cases on cookie sheets.

*2* Put the butter and sugar in a bowl and beat together until light and fluffy. Gradually beat in the egg. Sift in the flour and cocoa and then, using a metal spoon, fold them into the mixture. Stir in the milk. Fill a pastry bag, fitted with a large plain tip, with the batter and pipe it into the paper cases, filling each one until half full.

*3* Bake the cakes in a preheated oven, 375°F/190°C, for 10–15 minutes, or until well risen and firm to the touch. Transfer to a wire rack to cool.

*4* To make the frosting, break the chocolate into a pan and add the cream. Heat gently, stirring all the time, until the chocolate has melted. Pour into a large heatproof bowl and, using an electric hand whisk, beat the mixture for 10 minutes, or until thick, glossy and cool.

*5* Fill a pastry bag, fitted with a large star tip, with the frosting and pipe a swirl on top of each cupcake. Alternatively, spoon over the frosting. Chill in the refrigerator for 1 hour before serving. Serve decorated with a chocolate-coated coffee bean, if liked.

# dark & white chocolate fudge cakes

## ingredients

*makes 20*

7 fl oz/200 ml/generous
    ¾ cup water
3 oz/85 g/6 tbsp butter
3 oz/85 g/½ cup superfine sugar
1 tbsp dark corn syrup
3 tbsp milk
1 tsp vanilla extract
1 tsp baking soda
8 oz/225 g/1⅔ cups all-purpose
    flour
2 tbsp unsweetened cocoa

### topping

1¾ oz/50 g semisweet chocolate,
    broken into pieces
4 tbsp water
1¾ oz/50 g/3½ tbsp butter
1¾ oz/50 g white chocolate,
    broken into pieces
3 cups confectioners' sugar
3½ oz/100 g semisweet chocolate
    shavings and 3½ oz/100 g
    white chocolate shavings,
    for decorating

## method

1 Put 20 paper baking cases in muffin pans or or place 20 double-layer paper cases on cookie sheets.

2 Place the water, butter, sugar, and syrup in a saucepan and heat gently, stirring, until the sugar has dissolved. Bring to a boil, reduce the heat, and cook gently for 5 minutes. Let cool. Meanwhile, place the milk and vanilla extract in a bowl. Add the baking soda and stir to dissolve. Sift the flour and cocoa into a separate bowl and add the syrup mixture. Stir in the milk mixture and beat until smooth, then spoon the batter into the paper cases. Bake in a preheated oven, 350°F/180°C, for 20 minutes, or until well risen and firm to the touch. Transfer to a wire rack to cool.

3 To make the frosting, place the semisweet chocolate in a small heatproof bowl, add half the water and half the butter, set the bowl over a saucepan of gently simmering water, and heat until melted. Stir until smooth and then let stand over the water. Repeat with the white chocolate and remaining water and butter. Sift half the confectioners' sugar into each bowl and beat until smooth and thick.

4 When the cupcakes are cold, top alternately with each frosting, then let set. Decorate with chocolate shavings.

# chocolate cherry cupcakes

## ingredients

### makes 12

1¾ oz/50 g semisweet chocolate, broken into pieces
2¼ oz/65 g/4½ tbsp butter
4 oz/115 g/⅓ cup cherry jam
2½ oz/60 g/⅓ cup superfine sugar
2 large eggs
3½ oz/100 g/¾ cup self-rising flour

### topping

4 tsp Kirsch liqueur
⅔ cup heavy cream
12 fresh, candied, or maraschino cherries
chocolate curls, for decorating

## method

1 Put 12 paper baking cases in a muffin pan or place 12 double-layer paper cases on a cookie sheet.

2 Place the chocolate and butter in a saucepan and heat gently, stirring continuously, until melted. Pour into a large bowl, then stir until smooth and let cool slightly. Add the jam, sugar, and eggs to the cooled chocolate and beat together. Add the flour and stir together until combined. Spoon the batter into the paper cases.

3 Bake in a preheated oven, 350°F/180°C, for 20 minutes, or until firm to the touch. Let cool in the pan for 10 minutes, then transfer to a wire rack to cool completely.

4 When the cupcakes are cold, sprinkle the Kirsch over the tops of each and let soak for at least 15 minutes.

5 When ready to decorate, place the cream in a bowl and whip until soft peaks form. Spread the cream on top of the cupcakes with a knife to form the cream into peaks. Top each cupcake with a cherry and decorate with chocolate curls. Store the cupcakes in the refrigerator until ready to serve.

# chocolate fruit & nut crispy cakes

## ingredients

### makes 18

10½ oz/300 g semisweet
    chocolate, broken into pieces
5½ oz/150 g/generous ⅔ cup
    butter, cut into cubes
9 oz/250 g/¾ cup dark corn syrup
3½ oz/100 g/⅔ cup Brazil nuts,
    coarsely chopped
3½ oz/100 g/⅔ cup plumped
    dried raisins
7 oz/200 g/7 cups cornflakes
18 candied cherries, for decorating

## method

1 Place 18 paper baking cases in muffin pans or place
18 double-layer paper cases on cookie sheets.

2 Place the chocolate, butter, and dark corn syrup into a
large saucepan and heat gently until the butter has
melted and the ingredients are runny but not hot.
Remove from the heat and stir until well mixed.

3 Add the chopped nuts and raisins to the pan and
stir together until the fruit and nuts are covered in
chocolate. Add the cornflakes and stir until combined.

4 Spoon the mixture evenly into the paper cases and top
each with a candied cherry. Let set in a cool place for
2–4 hours before serving.

# chocolate butterfly cakes

## ingredients

*makes 12*

4 oz/115 g/½ cup soft margarine
3½ oz/100 g/½ cup superfine sugar
5½ oz/150 g/generous
    1½ cups self-rising white flour
2 large eggs
2 tbsp unsweetened cocoa
1 oz/25 g semisweet chocolate,
    melted
confectioners' sugar, for dusting

## filling

6 tbsp butter, softened
6 oz/175 g/1½ cups
    confectioners' sugar
1 oz/25 g semisweet chocolate,
    melted

## method

1 Put 12 paper baking cases in a muffin pan, or put 12 double-layer paper cases on a cookie sheet.

2 Put the margarine, sugar, flour, eggs, and cocoa in a large bowl and, using an electric hand whisk, beat together until just smooth. Beat in the melted chocolate. Spoon the batter into the paper cases, filling them three-fourths full.

3 Bake the cupcakes in a preheated oven, 350°F/180°C, for 15 minutes, or until springy to the touch. Transfer to a wire rack and let cool completely.

4 To make the filling, put the butter in a bowl and beat until fluffy. Sift in the confectioners' sugar and beat together until smooth. Add the melted chocolate and beat until well mixed.

5 When the cupcakes are cold, use a serrated knife to cut a circle from the top of each cake and then cut each circle in half. Spread or pipe a little of the buttercream into the center of each cupcake and press the 2 semicircular halves into it at an angle to resemble butterfly wings. Dust with sifted confectioners' sugar before serving.

# dark chocolate & ginger muffins

## ingredients

*makes 12*

6 tbsp sunflower oil or 6 tbsp
     butter, melted and cooled,
     plus extra for greasing
8 oz/225 g/1²/₃ cups all-purpose
     flour
2 oz/55 g/½ cup unsweetened
     cocoa
1 tbsp baking powder
1 tbsp ground ginger
pinch of salt
4 oz/115 g/generous ½ cup dark
     brown sugar
3 pieces preserved ginger in syrup,
     finely chopped, plus 2 tbsp
     syrup from the jar
2 eggs
7½ fl oz/220 ml/generous
     ¾ cup milk

## method

1  Grease a 12-cup muffin pan. Sift together the flour,
   cocoa, baking powder, ground ginger, and salt into a
   large bowl. Stir in the sugar and finely chopped
   preserved ginger

2  Place the eggs in a large pitcher or bowl and beat
   lightly, then beat in the milk, oil, and ginger syrup.
   Make a well in the center of the dry ingredients and
   pour in the beaten liquid ingredients. Stir gently until
   just combined; do not overmix. Spoon the batter into
   the muffin cups.

3  Bake in a preheated oven, 400°F/200°C, for 20 minutes,
   or until well risen and firm to the touch. Let cool in the
   pan for 5 minutes, then serve warm or transfer to a wire
   rack to cool completely.

# rocky road chocolate muffins

## ingredients

*makes 12*

6 tbsp sunflower oil or 6 tbsp
  butter, melted and cooled,
  plus extra for greasing
8 oz/225 g/1²/₃ cups all-purpose
  flour
2 oz/55 g/½ cup unsweetened
  cocoa
1 tbsp baking powder
pinch of salt
4 oz/115 g/generous ½ cup
  superfine sugar
3½ oz/100 g/generous ½ cup
  white chocolate chips
1¾ oz/50 g white mini
  marshmallows, cut in half
2 eggs
9 fl oz/250 ml/generous 1 cup milk

## method

1 Grease a 12-hole muffin pan. Sift together the flour,
  cocoa, baking powder, and salt into a large bowl.
  Stir in the sugar, chocolate chips, and marshmallows.

2 Place the eggs in a large pitcher or bowl and beat
  lightly, then beat in the milk and oil. Make a well in the
  center of the dry ingredients and pour in the beaten
  liquid ingredients. Stir gently until just combined; do
  not overmix. Spoon the batter into the muffin pan.

3 Bake in a preheated oven, 400°F/200°C, for 20 minutes,
  or until risen and firm to the touch. Let cool in the pan
  for 5 minutes, then serve warm or transfer to a wire
  rack to cool completely.

# chocolate chip muffins

## ingredients

*makes 12*

1½ oz/45 g/3 tbsp soft margarine
7 oz/200 g/1 cup superfine
    sugar
2 large eggs
5 fl oz/150 ml/²⁄₃ cup whole
    plain yogurt
5 tbsp milk
10 oz/300 g/2 cups
    all-purpose flour
1 tsp baking soda
4 oz/115 g/1 cup semisweet
    chocolate chips

## method

**1** Line a 12-cup muffin pan with 12 muffin liners.

**2** Place the margarine and sugar in a mixing bowl and beat with a wooden spoon until light and fluffy. Beat in the eggs, yogurt, and milk until combined.

**3** Sift the flour and baking soda into the batter. Stir until just blended.

**4** Stir in the chocolate chips, then divide the batter evenly among the muffin liners and bake in a preheated oven, 400°F/200°C, for 25 minutes, or until risen and golden. Remove the muffins from the oven and let cool in the pan for 5 minutes, then place them on a wire rack to cool completely.

# spiced chocolate muffins

## ingredients

*makes 12*

3½ oz/100 g/7 tbsp butter, softened
5 oz/150 g/scant ¾ cup superfine sugar
4 oz/115 g/½ cup packed brown sugar
2 large eggs
5 fl oz/150 ml/⅔ cup sour cream
5 tbsp milk
9 oz/250 g/generous 1¾ cups all-purpose flour
1 tsp baking soda
2 tbsp unsweetened cocoa
1 tsp allspice
7 oz/200 g/generous 1 cup semisweet chocolate chips

## method

1 Line a 12-cup muffin pan with 12 muffin liners.

2 Place the butter, superfine sugar, and brown sugar in a bowl and beat well. Beat in the eggs, sour cream, and milk until thoroughly mixed. Sift the flour, baking soda, cocoa, and allspice into a separate bowl and stir into the mixture. Add the chocolate chips and mix together well. Divide the batter evenly among the muffin liners.

3 Bake the muffins in a preheated oven, 375°F/190°C, for 25–30 minutes.

4 Remove from the oven and let cool for 10 minutes. Place them on a wire rack and let cool completely. Store in an airtight container until required.

# double chocolate muffins

## ingredients

*makes 12*

7 oz/200 g/scant 1½ cups
    all-purpose flour
1 oz/25 g/⅓ cup unsweetened
    cocoa, plus extra for dusting
1 tbsp baking powder
1 tsp ground cinnamon
4 oz/115 g/generous ½ cup golden
    superfine sugar
6½ oz/185 g white chocolate,
    broken into pieces
2 large eggs
3½ fl oz/100 ml/generous
    ⅓ cup sunflower or peanut oil
7 fl oz/200 ml/1 cup milk

## method

1 Line a 12-cup muffin pan with 12 muffin liners. Sift the flour, cocoa, baking powder, and cinnamon into a large mixing bowl. Stir in the sugar and 4½ oz/125 g of the white chocolate.

2 Place the eggs and oil in a separate bowl and whisk until frothy, then gradually whisk in the milk. Stir into the dry ingredients until just blended. Divide the batter evenly among the muffin liners, filling each three-quarters full. Bake in a preheated oven, 400°F/ 200°C, for 20 minutes, or until well risen and springy to the touch. Remove the muffins from the oven, let cool in the pan for 2 minutes, then remove them and place them on a wire rack to cool completely.

3 Place the remaining white chocolate in a heatproof bowl, set the bowl over a pan of barely simmering water, and heat until melted. Spread over the top of the muffins. Let set, then dust the tops with a little cocoa and serve.

# chocolate orange muffins

## ingredients

*makes 9*

sunflower or peanut oil,
   for oiling
5 oz/150 g/scant 1 cup
   self-rising white flour
5 oz/150 g/scant 1 cup self-rising
   whole wheat flour
2 oz/55 g/generous ¼ cup
   ground almonds
2 oz/55 g/generous ¼ cup packed
   brown sugar
rind and juice of 1 orange
6 oz/175 g/¾ cup cream cheese
2 large eggs
2 oz/55 g/⅓ cup semisweet
   chocolate chips

## method

1 Thoroughly oil a 9-cup muffin pan. Sift both flours into a mixing bowl and stir in the ground almonds and sugar.

2 Mix the orange rind and juice, cream cheese, and eggs together in a separate bowl. Make a well in the center of the dry ingredients and stir in the wet ingredients, then add the chocolate chips. Beat well to combine all the ingredients.

3 Divide the batter among the cups, filling each no more than three-quarters full. Bake in a preheated oven, 375°F/190°C, for 20–25 minutes until well risen and golden brown.

4 Remove the muffins from the oven and let cool slightly on a wire rack, but eat them as fresh as possible.

# mocha brownies

## ingredients

### makes 16

2 oz/55 g/4 tbsp butter, plus extra
   for greasing
4 oz/115 g semisweet chocolate,
   broken into pieces
6 oz/175 g/scant 1 cup
   brown sugar
2 eggs
1 tbsp instant coffee powder,
   dissolved in 1 tbsp hot
   water, cooled
3 oz/85 g/scant ⅔ cup
   all-purpose flour
½ tsp baking powder
2 oz/55 g/⅓ cup coarsely
   chopped pecans

## method

1 Grease and line the bottom of an 8-inch/20-cm
   square cake pan. Place the butter and chocolate in a
   heavy-bottom pan over low heat until melted. Stir and
   let cool.

2 Place the sugar and eggs in a large bowl and cream
   together until light and fluffy. Fold in the chocolate
   mixture and cooled coffee and mix thoroughly. Sift in
   the flour and baking powder and lightly fold into the
   mixture, then carefully fold in the pecans.

3 Pour the batter into the prepared pan and bake in a
   preheated oven, 350°F/180°C, for 25–30 minutes, or
   until firm and a skewer inserted into the center comes
   out clean.

4 Let cool in the pan for a few minutes, then run a knife
   round the edge of the cake to loosen it. Turn the cake
   out onto a wire rack and peel off the lining paper. Let
   cool completely. When cold, cut into squares.

# cappuccino squares

## ingredients

*makes 15*

8 oz/225 g/1 cup butter, softened,
    plus extra for greasing
8 oz/225 g/generous
    1½ cups self-rising flour
1 tsp baking powder
1 tsp unsweetened cocoa,
    plus extra for dusting
8 oz/225 g/generous 1 cup
    golden superfine sugar
4 eggs, beaten
3 tbsp instant coffee powder,
    dissolved in 2 tbsp hot water

### frosting

4 oz/115 g white chocolate,
    broken into pieces
2 oz/55 g butter, softened
3 tbsp milk
6 oz/175 g/1¾ cups
    confectioners' sugar

## method

1 Grease and line the bottom of a shallow 11 x 7-inch/
28 x 18-cm pan. Sift the flour, baking powder, and
cocoa into a bowl and add the butter, superfine sugar,
eggs, and coffee. Beat well, by hand or with an electric
whisk, until smooth, then spoon into the pan and
smooth the top.

2 Bake in a preheated oven, 350°F/180°C, for 35–40
minutes, or until risen and firm. Let cool in the pan
for 10 minutes, then turn out onto a wire rack and peel
off the lining paper. Let cool completely.

3 To make the frosting, place the chocolate, butter, and
milk in a bowl set over a pan of simmering water and
stir until the chocolate has melted. Remove the bowl
from the pan and sift in the confectioners' sugar. Beat
until smooth, then spread over the cake. Dust the top
of the cake with sifted cocoa, then cut into squares.

# chocolate tartlets

## ingredients

*makes 4*

10 oz/275 g ready-made sweet
    pie dough
5½ oz/150 g bittersweet chocolate,
    broken into pieces
1¾ oz/50 g/3½ tbsp butter
3½ fl oz/100 ml/scant ½ cup
    whipping cream
1 large egg
1 oz/30 g/scant ⅛ cup superfine
    sugar
unsweetened cocoa and chocolate
    curls, to decorate
crème fraîche, to serve

## method

1  Roll out the pie dough and use to line 4 x 4½-inch/
   12-cm fluted tart pans with removable bases. Line the
   pastry shells with parchment paper, then fill with dried
   beans. Place on a preheated cookie sheet and bake in
   a preheated oven, 400°F/200°C, for 5 minutes, or until
   the pastry rims look set. Remove the paper and beans
   and return the pastry shells to the oven for 5 minutes,
   or until the bases look dry. Remove from the oven,
   then let stand on the cookie sheet. Reduce the oven
   temperature to 350°F/180°C.

2  Meanwhile, place the chocolate in a bowl set over
   a pan of simmering water, without the bowl touching
   the water. Add the butter and cream and heat until
   the chocolate and butter melt. Remove from the heat.

3  Beat the egg and sugar together until light and fluffy.
   Stir the melted chocolate mixture until smooth, then
   stir it into the egg mixture. Carefully pour the filling
   into the tart shells, then transfer to the oven and bake
   for 15 minutes, or until the filling is set and the pastry
   is golden brown. If the pastry looks as though it is
   becoming too brown, cover it with foil.

4  Transfer the tartlets to a wire rack to cool completely.
   Dust with unsweetened cocoa, decorate with
   chocolate curls, and serve with crème fraîche.

# caramel chocolate shortbread

## ingredients

*makes 12*

4 oz/115 g/8 tbsp butter, plus
    extra for greasing
6 oz/175 g/¾ cup all-purpose flour
2 oz/55 g/⅓ cup superfine sugar

### filling and topping

6 oz/175 g butter
4 oz/115 g/²/₃ cup superfine sugar
3 tbsp dark corn syrup
14 oz/400 g canned condensed
    milk
7 oz/200 g semisweet chocolate,
    broken into pieces

## method

1 Grease and line the bottom of a 9-inch/23-cm shallow square cake pan. Place the butter, flour, and sugar in a food processor and process until it starts to bind together. Press into the pan and level the top. Bake in a preheated oven, 350°F/180°C, for 20–25 minutes, or until golden.

2 Meanwhile, make the caramel. Place the butter, sugar, syrup, and condensed milk in a heavy-bottom pan. Heat gently until the sugar has melted. Bring to a boil, then reduce the heat and let simmer for 6–8 minutes, stirring, until very thick. Pour over the shortbread and let chill in the refrigerator for 2 hours, or until firm.

3 Melt the chocolate and let cool, then spread over the caramel. Let chill in the refrigerator for 2 hours, or until set. Cut the shortbread into 12 pieces using a sharp knife and serve.

# double chocolate chip cookies

## ingredients

*makes 12*

7 oz/200 g/scant 1 cup butter, softened, plus extra for greasing
7 oz/200 g/1 cup golden superfine sugar
½ tsp vanilla extract
1 large egg
8 oz/225 g/1½ cups all-purpose flour
pinch of salt
1 tsp baking soda
4 oz/115 g/⅔ cup white chocolate chips
4 oz/115 g/⅔ cup semisweet chocolate chips

## method

1 Place the butter, sugar, and vanilla extract in a large bowl and beat together. Gradually beat in the egg until the mixture is light and fluffy.

2 Sift the flour, salt, and baking soda over the mixture and fold in. Fold in the chocolate chips. Drop dessertspoonfuls of the mixture onto 3 greased cookie sheets, spaced well apart to allow for spreading during cooking.

3 Bake in a preheated oven, 350°F/180°C, for 10–12 minutes, or until crisp outside but still soft inside. Let cool on the cookie sheets for 2 minutes, then transfer to wire racks to cool completely.

# special
# occasions

# easter cupcakes

## ingredients

### makes 12

4 oz/115 g/½ cup butter, softened, or soft margarine
4 oz/115 g/generous ½ cup superfine sugar
2 eggs, lightly beaten
3 oz/85 g/generous ½ cup self-rising white flour
1 oz/25 g/generous ¼ cup unsweetened cocoa

## topping

3 oz/85 g/6 tbsp butter, softened
6 oz/175 g/1½ cups confectioners' sugar
1 tbsp milk
2–3 drops of vanilla extract
36 mini chocolate candy shell eggs, to decorate

## method

*1* Put 12 paper baking cases in a muffin pan, or place 12 double-layer paper cases on a cookie sheet.

*2* Put the butter and sugar in a bowl and beat together until light and fluffy. Gradually add the eggs, beating well after each addition. Sift in the flour and cocoa and, using a large metal spoon, fold into the mixture. Spoon the batter into the paper cases.

*3* Bake the cupcakes in a preheated oven, 350°F/180°C, for 15–20 minutes, or until well risen and firm to the touch. Transfer to a wire rack and let cool.

*4* To make the buttercream topping, put the butter in a bowl and beat until fluffy. Sift in the confectioners' sugar and beat together until well mixed, adding the milk and vanilla extract.

*5* When the cupcakes are cold, put the frosting in a pastry bag, fitted with a large star tip, and pipe a circle around the edge of each cupcake to form a nest. Place 3 chocolate eggs in the center of each nest, to decorate.

# springtime cupcakes

## ingredients

*makes 24*

5½ oz/150 g/⅔ cup butter,
    softened, or soft margarine
5½ oz/150 g/¾ cup superfine sugar
1 tsp vanilla extract
2 large eggs, lightly beaten
5 oz/140 g/1 cup self-rising flour
1½ oz/40 g/generous ¼ cup
    cornstarch

### topping

4 oz/115 g ready-to-roll fondant
yellow and green food colorings
10½ oz/300 g/2⅔ cups
    confectioners' sugar
about 3 tbsp cold water
colored sprinkles

## method

1  Place 24 paper baking cases in muffin pans or place 24 double-layer paper cases on a cookie sheet.

2  Place the butter and sugar in a large bowl and beat together until light and fluffy, then beat in the vanilla extract. Gradually beat in the eggs. Sift in the flour and cornstarch and fold into the batter. Spoon the batter into the paper cases. Bake in a preheated oven, 375°F/ 190°C, for 12–15 minutes, or until golden and springy to the touch. Transfer to a wire rack to cool completely.

3  To decorate, divide the fondant in half and color one half pale yellow. Roll out both halves, then use the sides of a round cookie cutter to cut out white and yellow petal shapes. Set aside.

4  Sift the confectioners' sugar into a bowl and mix with the water until smooth. Place half of the icing in a small pastry bag fitted with a small plain tip. Divide the remaining icing in half and color one portion yellow and the other green.

5  Cover 12 cakes with yellow icing and 12 with green icing. Arrange petals on top of the icing to form flowers. Pipe a little blob of white icing into the center of each flower, then add a few colored sprinkles on top of the white icing to form the center of the flower. Let set.

# halloween cupcakes

## ingredients

*makes 12*

4 oz/115 g/½ cup soft margarine
4 oz/115 g/generous ½ cup
    superfine sugar
2 eggs
4 oz/115 g/generous ¾ cup
    self-rising white flour

### topping

7 oz/200 g orange ready-to-roll
    colored fondant frosting
confectioners' sugar, for dusting
2 oz/55 g black ready-to-roll
    colored fondant frosting
black cake writing frosting
white cake writing frosting

## method

*1* Put 12 paper baking cases in a muffin pan, or place
    12 double-layer paper cases on a cookie sheet.

*2* Put the margarine, sugar, eggs, and flour in a bowl
    and, using an electric hand whisk, beat together until
    smooth. Spoon the batter into the paper cases.

*3* Bake the cupcakes in a preheated oven, 350°F/180°C,
    for 15–20 minutes, or until well risen, golden brown,
    and firm to the touch. Transfer to a wire rack and
    let cool.

*4* Knead the orange frosting until pliable, then roll out on
    a counter dusted with confectioners' sugar. Using the
    palm of your hand, lightly rub confectioners' sugar
    into the frosting to prevent it from spotting. Using a
    2¼-inch/5.5-cm plain round cutter, cut out 12 circles,
    re-rolling the frosting as necessary. Place a circle on
    top of each cupcake.

*5* Roll out the black frosting on a counter lightly dusted
    with confectioners' sugar. Using the palm of your hand,
    lightly rub confectioners' sugar into the frosting to
    prevent it from spotting. Using a 1¼-inch/3-cm plain
    round cutter, cut out 12 circles and place them on the
    center of the cupcakes. Using black writing frosting,
    pipe 8 legs on to each spider and using white writing
    frosting, draw 2 eyes and a mouth.

# christmas cupcakes

## ingredients

### makes 16

4½ oz/130 g/generous 1 cup
  butter, softened
7 oz/200 g/1 cup superfine sugar
4–6 drops almond extract
4 eggs, lightly beaten
5½ oz/150 g/generous 1 cup
  self-rising white flour
6 oz/175 g/1¾ cups ground
  almonds

### topping

1 lb/450 g white ready-to-roll
  fondant frosting
2 oz/55 g green ready-to-roll
  colored fondant frosting
1 oz/25 g red ready-to-roll colored
  fondant frosting
confectioners' sugar, for dusting

## method

1 Place 16 paper baking cases in muffin pans or place 16 double-layer paper cases on cookie sheets.

2 Put the butter, sugar, and almond extract in a bowl and beat together until light and fluffy. Gradually add the eggs, beating well after each addition. Add the flour and, using a large metal spoon, fold it into the mixture, then fold in the ground almonds. Spoon the batter into the paper cases to half-fill them.

3 Bake the cakes in a preheated oven, 350°F/180°C, for 20 minutes, or until well risen, golden brown, and firm to the touch. Transfer to a wire rack and let cool. When the cakes are cold, knead the white frosting until pliable, then roll out on a counter lightly dusted with confectioners' sugar. Using a 2¾-inch/7-cm plain round cutter, cut out 16 circles, re-rolling the frosting as necessary. Place a circle on top of each cupcake.

4 Roll out the green frosting on a counter lightly dusted with confectioners' sugar. Using the palm of your hand, rub confectioners' sugar into the frosting to prevent it from spotting. Using a holly leaf-shaped cutter, cut out 32 leaves, rerolling as necessary. Brush each leaf with a little cooled water and place 2 leaves on top of each cake. Roll the red frosting between your hands to form 48 berries and place in the center of the leaves.

# valentine heart cupcakes

## ingredients

*makes 6*

3 oz/85 g/6 tbsp butter, softened, or soft margarine
3 oz/85 g/scant ½ cup superfine sugar
½ tsp vanilla extract
2 eggs, lightly beaten
2½ oz/70 g/½ cup all-purpose flour
1 tbsp unsweetened cocoa
1 tsp baking powder

### marzipan hearts

1¼ oz/35 g marzipan
red food coloring (liquid or paste)
confectioners' sugar, for dusting

### topping

2 oz/60 g/4 tbsp butter, softened
4 oz/115 g/1 cup confectioners' sugar
1 oz/25 g semisweet chocolate, melted
6 chocolate flower decorations

## method

1 To make the hearts, knead the marzipan until pliable, then add a few drops of red coloring and knead until evenly colored red. Roll out the marzipan to a thickness of ¼ inch/5 mm on a counter dusted with confectioners' sugar. Using a small heart-shaped cutter, cut out 6 hearts. Place on a tray lined with waxed paper and dusted with confectioners' sugar. Let the hearts dry for 3–4 hours.

2 Place 6 paper baking cases in a muffin pan.

3 Put the butter, sugar, and vanilla extract in a bowl and beat together until light and fluffy. Gradually add the eggs, beating well after each addition. Sift in the flour, cocoa, and baking powder and, using a large metal spoon, fold into the mixture. Spoon the batter into the paper cases.

4 Bake the cupcakes in a preheated oven, 350°F/180°C, for 20–25 minutes, or until well risen and firm to the touch. Transfer to a wire rack and let cool.

5 To make the topping, put the butter in a large bowl and beat until fluffy. Sift in the confectioners' sugar and beat together until smooth. Add the melted chocolate and beat together until well mixed. When the cakes are cold, spread the frosting on top of each cake and decorate with a marzipan heart and a chocolate flower.

# cupcake wedding cake

## ingredients

### makes 48

1 lb/450 g/2 cups butter, softened
1 lb/450 g/2 cups superfine sugar
2 tsp vanilla extract
8 large eggs, lightly beaten
1 lb/450 g/4 cups self-rising
    white flour
5 fl oz/150 ml/²/₃ cup milk

### topping

1 lb 4 oz/550 g/5 cups
    confectioners' sugar
48 ready-made sugar roses,
    or 48 small fresh rosebuds
    gently rinsed and left to dry
    on paper towels

### to assemble the cake

one 20-inch/50-cm, one
    16-inch/40-cm, one
    12-inch/30-cm, and one
    8-inch/20-cm sandblasted
    glass disk with polished edges,
    or 4 silver cake boards
13 white or Perspex cake pillars
1 small bouquet of fresh flowers in
    a small vase

## method

*1* Put 48 paper baking cases in muffin pans, or place 48 double-layer paper cases on cookie sheets.

*2* Put the butter, sugar, and vanilla extract in a bowl and beat together until light and fluffy. Gradually add the eggs, beating well after each addition. Add the flour and, using a large metal spoon, fold into the mixture with the milk. Spoon the batter into the paper cases.

*3* Bake the cupcakes in a preheated oven, 350°F/180°C, for 15–20 minutes, or until well risen and firm to the touch. Transfer to a wire rack and let cool.

*4* To make the topping, sift the confectioners' sugar into a large bowl. Add 3–4 tablespoons hot water and stir until the mixture is smooth and thick enough to coat the back of a wooden spoon. Spoon on top of each cupcake. Store in an airtight container for up to one day.

*5* On the day of serving, carefully place a sugar rose or rosebud on top of each cupcake. To arrange the cupcakes, place the largest disk or board on a table where the finished display is to be. Stand 5 pillars on the disk and arrange some of the cupcakes on the base. Continue with the remaining bases, pillars (using only 4 pillars to support each remaining tier), and cupcakes to make 4 tiers, standing the bouquet of flowers in the center of the top tier.

# rose petal cupcakes

## ingredients

*makes 12*

4 oz/115 g/½ cup butter, softened
4 oz/115 g/generous ½ cup
    superfine sugar
2 eggs, lightly beaten
1 tbsp milk
few drops of extract of rose oil
¼ tsp vanilla extract
6 oz/175 g/scant 1¼ cups
    self-rising white flour

### topping

3 oz/85 g/6 tbsp butter, softened
6 oz/175 g/1½ cups
    confectioners' sugar
pink or purple food coloring
    (optional)
silver dragées (cake decoration
    balls), to decorate

### candied rose petals

12–24 rose petals
lightly beaten egg white,
    for brushing
superfine sugar, for sprinkling

## method

**1** To make the candied rose petals, gently rinse the petals and dry well with paper towels. Using a pastry brush, paint both sides of a rose petal with egg white, then coat well with superfine sugar. Place on a tray and repeat with the remaining petals. Cover the tray with foil and let dry overnight.

**2** Put 12 paper baking cases in a muffin pan, or place 12 double-layer paper cases on a cookie sheet.

**3** Put the butter and sugar in a bowl and beat together until light and fluffy. Gradually add the eggs, beating well after each addition. Stir in the milk, rose oil extract, and vanilla extract then, using a metal spoon, fold in the flour. Spoon the batter into the paper cases.

**4** Bake the cupcakes in a preheated oven, 400°F/200°C, for 12–15 minutes until well risen and golden brown. Transfer to a wire rack and let cool.

**5** To make the frosting, put the butter in a large bowl and beat until fluffy. Sift in the confectioners' sugar and mix well together. If wished, add a few drops of pink or purple food coloring to complement the rose petals.

**6** When the cupcakes are cold, spread the frosting on top of each cake. Top with 1–2 candied rose petals and sprinkle with silver dragées to decorate.

# lemon butterfly cakes

## ingredients

### makes 12

4 oz/115 g/generous ¾ cup
    self-rising white flour
½ tsp baking powder
8 tbsp soft margarine
4 oz/115 g/generous ½ cup
    superfine sugar
2 eggs, lightly beaten
finely grated rind of ½ lemon
2 tbsp milk
confectioners' sugar, for dusting

### filling

3 oz/85 g/6 tbsp butter, softened
6 oz/175 g/1½ cups
    confectioners' sugar
1 tbsp lemon juice

## method

1 Put 12 paper baking cases in a muffin pan, or place 12 double-layer paper cases on a cookie sheet.

2 Sift the flour and baking powder into a large bowl. Add the margarine, sugar, eggs, lemon rind, and milk and, using an electric hand whisk, beat together until smooth. Spoon the batter into the paper cases. Bake the cupcakes in a preheated oven, 375°F/190°C, for 15–20 minutes, or until well risen and golden brown. Transfer to a wire rack and let cool.

3 To make the filling, put the butter in a bowl and beat until fluffy. Sift in the confectioners' sugar, add the lemon juice, and beat together until smooth and creamy.

4 When the cupcakes are cold, use a serrated knife to cut a circle from the top of each cupcake and then cut each circle in half. Spread or pipe a little of the buttercream filling into the center of each cupcake, then press the 2 semicircular halves into it at an angle to resemble butterfly wings. Dust with sifted confectioners' sugar before serving.

## variation

Omit the lemon rind from the cake mixture and replace the lemon juice in the frosting with 1 tsp of vanilla extract.

# baby shower cupcakes

## ingredients

*makes 24*

14 oz/400 g/1¾ cups
    butter, softened
14 oz/400 g/2 cups
    superfine sugar
finely grated rind of 2 lemons
8 eggs, lightly beaten
14 oz/400 g/generous
    2¾ cups self-rising white flour

## topping

12 oz/350 g/3 cups
    confectioners' sugar
red or blue food coloring
    (liquid or paste)
24 sugared almonds

## method

*1* Put 24 paper baking cases in muffin pans, or 24 double-layer paper cases on cookie sheets.

*2* Put the butter, sugar, and lemon rind in a bowl and beat together until light and fluffy. Gradually add the eggs, beating well after each addition. Add the flour and, using a large metal spoon, fold into the mixture. Spoon the batter into the paper cases to half-fill them.

*3* Bake the cupcakes in a preheated oven, 350°F/180°C, for 20–25 minutes, or until well risen, golden brown, and firm to the touch. Transfer to a wire rack and let cool.

*4* When the cakes are cold, make the topping. Sift the confectioners' sugar into a bowl. Add 6–8 teaspoons of hot water and stir until the mixture is smooth and thick enough to coat the back of a wooden spoon. Dip a skewer into the red or blue food coloring, then stir it into the frosting until it is evenly colored pink or pale blue.

*5* Spoon the frosting on top of each cupcake. Top each with a sugared almond and let set for about 30 minutes before serving.

# birthday party cupcakes

## ingredients

*makes 24*

8 oz/225 g/1 cup soft margarine
8 oz/225 g/scant 1¼ cups
    superfine sugar
4 eggs
8 oz/225 g/generous
    1½ cups self-rising white flour

### topping

6 oz/175 g/¾ cup butter, softened
12 oz/350 g/3 cups confectioners'
    sugar
a variety of edible sugar flower
    shapes, cake decorating
    sprinkles, silver dragées
    (cake decoration balls),
    and sugar strands
various colored tubes of writing
    frosting
24 birthday cake candles
    (optional)
silver dragées (cake decoration
    balls)

## method

*1* Put 24 paper baking cases in muffin pans, or place 24 double-layer paper cases on cookie sheets.

*2* Put the margarine, sugar, eggs, and flour in a large bowl and, using an electric hand whisk, beat together until just smooth. Spoon the batter into the paper cases.

*3* Bake the cupcakes in a preheated oven, 350°F/180°C, for 15–20 minutes, or until well risen, golden brown, and firm to the touch. Transfer to a wire rack and let cool.

*4* To make the frosting, put the butter in a bowl and beat until fluffy. Sift in the confectioners' sugar and beat together until smooth and creamy. When the cupcakes are cold, spread the frosting on top of each cupcake, then decorate to your choice and, if desired, place a candle in the top of each.

# gold & silver anniversary cupcakes

## ingredients

### makes 24

8 oz/225 g/1 cup butter, softened
8 oz/225 g/generous 1 cup
    superfine sugar
1 tsp vanilla extract
4 large eggs, lightly beaten
8 oz/225 g/generous 1½ cups
    self-rising white flour
5 tbsp milk

## topping

6 oz/175 g/¾ cup unsalted butter
12 oz/350 g/3 cups
    confectioners' sugar
silver or gold dragées
    (cake decoration balls)

## method

**1** Put 24 paper baking cases in muffin pans, or place
    24 double-layer paper cases on cookie sheets.

**2** Put the butter, sugar, and vanilla extract in a bowl and
    beat together until light and fluffy. Gradually add the
    eggs, beating well after each addition. Add the flour
    and, using a large metal spoon, fold into the mixture
    with the milk. Spoon the batter into the paper cases.

**3** Bake the cupcakes in a preheated oven, 350°F/180°C,
    for 15–20 minutes, or until well risen and firm to the
    touch. Transfer to a wire rack and let cool.

**4** To make the topping, put the butter in a large bowl
    and beat until fluffy. Sift in the confectioners' sugar
    and beat together until well mixed. Put the topping
    in a pastry bag, fitted with a medium star-shaped tip.

**5** When the cupcakes are cold, pipe icing on top of each.
    Sprinkle over the silver or gold dragées before serving.

# lavender fairy cakes

## ingredients

### makes 12

4 oz/115 g/generous ½ cup
    golden superfine sugar
4 oz/115 g butter, softened
2 eggs, beaten
1 tbsp milk
1 tsp finely chopped lavender
    flowers
½ tsp vanilla extract
6 oz/175 g/1¼ cups self-rising
    flour, sifted
5 oz/150 g/scant 1½ cups
    confectioners' sugar

### to decorate
lavender flowers
silver dragées (cake
    decoration balls)

## method

1 Put 12 paper baking cases in a muffin pan or place 12 double-layer paper cases on a cookie sheet.

2 Place the superfine sugar and butter in a bowl and cream together until pale and fluffy. Gradually beat in the eggs. Stir in the milk, lavender, and vanilla extract, then carefully fold in the flour.

3 Divide the mixture among the paper cases and bake in a preheated oven, 400°F/200°C, for 12–15 minutes, or until well risen and golden. The sponge should bounce back when pressed.

4 A few minutes before the cakes are ready, sift the confectioners' sugar into a bowl and stir in enough water to make a thick frosting.

5 When the fairy cakes are baked, transfer to a wire rack and place a blob of frosting in the center of each one, allowing it to run across the cake. Decorate with lavender flowers and silver dragées and serve as soon as the cakes are cool.

# iced cupcakes

## ingredients

*makes 12*

4 oz/115 g/½ cup butter, softened
4 oz/115 g/½ cup superfine sugar
2 eggs, lightly beaten
4 oz/115 g/generous ¾ cup
    self-rising flour

## topping

7 oz/200 g/1¾ cups
    confectioners' sugar
about 2 tbsp warm water
a few drops of food coloring
    (optional)
sugar flowers, colored sprinkles,
    candied cherries, and/or
    chocolate strands,
    for decorating

## method

1 Put 12 paper baking cases in a muffin pan, or place 12 double-layer paper cases on a cookie sheet.

2 Place the butter and sugar in a large bowl and beat together until light and fluffy, then gradually beat in the eggs. Sift in the flour and fold into the mixture. Spoon the batter into the paper cases.

3 Bake in a preheated oven, 375°F/190°C, for 15–20 minutes. Transfer to a wire rack to cool completely.

4 To make the icing, sift the confectioners' sugar into a bowl and stir in just enough warm water to mix to a smooth paste that is thick enough to coat the back of a wooden spoon. Stir in a few drops of food coloring, if using, then spread the icing over the cupcakes and decorate, as liked.

# boutique cupcakes

## ingredients

### *makes 10*

6 oz/175 g/¾ cup butter, softened,
    or soft margarine
6 oz/175 g/1 cup superfine sugar
1 tsp vanilla extract
3 eggs, lightly beaten
5 oz/150 g/1¼ cups raspberries
8 oz/225 g/1⅔ cups self-rising
    flour

### topping

8 oz/225 g/1 cup butter, softened
1 tbsp cream or milk
12 oz/350 g/generous 3 cups
    confectioners' sugar
pink, black, red, and yellow
    food coloring
2–3 oz/55–85 g ready-to-roll
    fondant
silver dragées (cake
    decoration balls)
gummy candies

## method

1 Put 10 paper baking cases in a muffin pan, or place
    10 double-layer paper cases on a cookie sheet.

2 Place the butter and sugar in a large bowl and beat
    together until light and fluffy, then beat in the vanilla
    extract. Gradually beat in the eggs, then fold the
    raspberries and flour into the batter. Spoon the batter
    into the paper cases.

3 Bake in a preheated oven, 180°F/350°C, for 20–25
    minutes, or until golden brown and springy to the
    touch. Transfer to a wire rack to cool completely.

4 To make the buttercream, place the butter and cream
    in a bowl and beat together. Gradually sift in the icing
    sugar and beat until smooth.

5 To decorate, color the buttercream pale pink, then
    place in a pastry bag fitted with a large star tip and
    pipe the buttercream on top of the cakes.

6 Color the fondant and then mold into different shapes,
    such as handbags, high-heeled shoes, or rings. Arrange
    the shapes on the cupcakes, then press silver dragées
    into the frosting to form the handle of the bag and to
    decorate the shoes. Use gummy candies to make the
    gems on the rings.

# rose petal muffins

## ingredients

*makes 12*

1 tbsp sunflower or peanut oil,
    for oiling (if using)
8 oz/225 g/1½ cups
    all-purpose flour
2 tsp baking powder
pinch of salt
4 tbsp butter
6 tbsp superfine sugar
1 large egg, beaten
4 fl oz/110 ml/½ cup milk
1 tsp rose water
1¾ oz/50 g edible rose petals,
    rinsed, patted dry, and lightly
    snipped

### topping
3½ oz/100 g/scant 1 cup
    confectioners' sugar
1 tbsp liquid glucose
1 tbsp rose water
1¾ oz/50 g edible rose petals,
    rinsed and patted dry

## method

1 Oil a 12-cup muffin pan with sunflower oil, or line it
    with 12 muffin liners. Sift the flour, baking powder, and
    salt into a large mixing bowl.

2 In a separate large bowl, cream together the butter and
    superfine sugar, then stir in the beaten egg, milk, rose
    water, and snipped rose petals. Add the butter mixture
    to the flour mixture and then gently stir together until
    just combined. Do not overstir the batter—it is fine for
    it to be a little lumpy.

3 Divide the muffin batter evenly among the 12 cups
    in the muffin pan or the muffin liners (they should be
    about two-thirds full). Transfer to a preheated oven,
    400°F/200°C, and bake for 20 minutes, or until risen
    and golden.

4 While the muffins are cooking, make the frosting. Place
    the confectioners' sugar in a bowl, then stir in the liquid
    glucose and rose water. Cover with plastic wrap until
    ready to use.

5 When the muffins are cooked, remove them from the
    oven, place on a wire rack, and let cool. When they
    have cooled, spread each muffin with some of the
    frosting, strew over and/or around with the rose petals,
    and serve.

# rose-topped wedding muffins

## ingredients

*makes 12*

10 oz/280 g/2 cups all-purpose
    flour
1 tbsp baking powder
pinch of salt
4 oz/115 g/generous ½ cup
    superfine sugar
2 eggs
generous 1 cup milk
6 tbsp sunflower oil or 6 tbsp
    butter, melted and cooled
1 tsp vanilla extract

### topping

6 oz/175 g/1½ cups
    confectioners' sugar
3–4 tsp hot water
12 store-bought sugar roses,
    for decorating

## method

*1* Increase the quantity of ingredients according to the number of wedding guests invited; double the quantities to make 24 muffins. Line the muffin pans with muffin liners.

*2* Sift together the flour, baking powder, and salt into a large bowl. Stir in the sugar. Place the eggs in a large pitcher or bowl and beat lightly, then beat in the milk, oil, and vanilla extract. Make a well in the center of the dry ingredients and pour in the beaten liquid ingredients. Stir gently until just combined; do not overmix. Spoon the batter into the muffin liners.

*3* Bake in a preheated oven, 400°F/200°C, for 20 minutes, or until well risen, golden brown, and firm to the touch. Let cool in the pan or pans for 5 minutes, then transfer to a wire rack to cool completely. Store in the freezer until required.

*4* For the icing, sift the confectioners' sugar into a bowl. Add the water and stir until the mixture is smooth and thick enough to coat the back of a wooden spoon. Spoon the icing on top of each muffin, then top with a sugar rose.

# mother's day breakfast muffins

## ingredients

*makes 12*

10 oz/280 g/2 cups all-purpose
    flour
1 tbsp baking powder
pinch of salt
4 oz/115 g/generous ½ cup
    superfine sugar
2 eggs
9 fl oz/250 ml/generous 1 cup milk
6 tbsp sunflower oil or 6 tbsp
    butter, melted and cooled
1 tsp orange extract
fresh strawberries, for serving
confectioners' sugar, for dusting

## method

*1* Line a 12-cup muffin pan with 12 muffin liners. Sift together the flour, baking powder, and salt into a large bowl. Stir in the superfine sugar.

*2* Place the eggs in a large pitcher or bowl and beat lightly, then beat in the milk, oil, and orange extract. Make a well in the center of the dry ingredients and pour in the beaten liquid ingredients. Stir gently until just combined; do not overmix. Spoon the batter into the muffin liners.

*3* Bake in a preheated oven, 400°F/200°C, for 20 minutes, or until well risen, golden brown, and firm to the touch. Let cool in the pan for 5 minutes. Meanwhile, arrange the strawberries in a bowl. Dust the muffins with sifted confectioners' sugar and serve warm.

# children's party muffins

## ingredients

### makes 12

10 oz/280 g/2 cups all-purpose flour
1 tbsp baking powder
½ tsp salt
4 oz/115 g/generous ½ cup superfine sugar
2 eggs
9 fl oz/250 ml/generous 1 cup milk
6 tbsp sunflower oil or 6 tbsp butter, melted and cooled
1 tsp vanilla extract

### topping

6 oz/175 g/1½ cups confectioners' sugar
3–4 tsp hot water
variety of small candies, for decorating

## method

1 Line a 12-cup muffin pan with 12 muffin liners. Sift together the flour, baking powder, and salt into a large bowl. Stir in the superfine sugar.

2 Place the eggs in a large pitcher or bowl and beat lightly, then beat in the milk, oil, and vanilla extract. Make a well in the center of the dry ingredients and pour in the beaten liquid ingredients. Stir until combined. Spoon the batter into the muffin liners.

3 Bake in a preheated oven, 400°F/200°C, for 20 minutes, or until well risen, golden brown, and firm to the touch. Let cool in the pan for 5 minutes, then transfer to a wire rack to cool completely.

4 When the muffins are cold, make the icing. Sift the confectioners' sugar into a bowl. Add the water and stir until the mixture is smooth and thick enough to coat the back of a wooden spoon. Spoon the icing on top of each muffin, then add the decoration of your choice. Let set for about 30 minutes before serving.

# mocha muffins

## ingredients

### makes 12

1 tbsp sunflower or peanut oil,
   for oiling (if using)
9 oz/250 g/generous 1¾ cups
   all-purpose flour
1 tbsp baking powder
2 tbsp unsweetened cocoa
pinch of salt
4 oz/115 g/½ cup butter, melted
5½ oz/150 g/scant ¾ cup raw
   brown sugar
1 large egg, beaten
4 fl oz/110 ml/1 cup milk
1 tsp almond extract
2 tbsp strong coffee
1 tbsp instant coffee powder
2 oz/115 g/generous ¼ cup
   semisweet chocolate chips
1 oz/25 g/scant ⅓ cup raisins

### topping

3 tbsp raw brown sugar
1 tbsp unsweetened cocoa
1 tsp allspice

## method

*1* Oil a 12-cup muffin pan with sunflower oil, or line
   it with 12 muffin liners. Sift the flour, baking powder,
   cocoa, and salt into a large mixing bowl

*2* In a separate large bowl, cream the butter and raw
   sugar together, then stir in the beaten egg. Pour in the
   milk, almond extract, and coffee, then add the coffee
   powder, chocolate chips, and raisins and gently mix
   together. Add the raisin mixture to the flour mixture
   and gently stir together until just combined. Do not
   overstir the batter—it is fine for it to be a little lumpy.

*3* Divide the muffin batter evenly among the 12 cups
   in the muffin pan or the muffin liners (they should be
   about two-thirds full). To make the topping, place the
   raw sugar in a bowl, add the cocoa and allspice, and
   mix together well.

*4* Sprinkle the topping over the muffins, then transfer
   to a preheated oven, 375°F/190°C, and bake for
   20 minutes, or until risen and golden. Remove the
   muffins from the oven and serve warm, or place them
   on a wire rack and let cool.

# marshmallow muffins

## ingredients

*makes 12*

2½ oz/70 g/5 tbsp butter
10 oz/275 g/2 cups
   all-purpose flour
6 tbsp unsweetened cocoa
3 tsp baking powder
3 oz/85 g/scant ½ cup
   superfine sugar
3½ oz/100 g/generous ½ cup milk
   chocolate chips
2 oz/55 g/¼ cup multicolored
   mini marshmallows
1 large egg, beaten
10 fl oz/300 ml/1¼ cups milk

## method

1 Line a 12-cup muffin pan with 12 muffin liners. Melt the butter in a pan. Sift the flour, cocoa, and baking powder together into a large bowl. Stir in the sugar, chocolate chips, and marshmallows until thoroughly mixed.

2 Whisk the egg, milk, and melted butter together in a separate bowl, then gently stir into the flour to form a stiff batter. Divide the batter evenly among the muffin liners.

3 Bake in a preheated oven, 375°F/190°C, for 20–25 minutes until well risen and golden brown. Remove from the oven and let cool in the pan for 5 minutes, then place on a wire rack and let cool completely.

# christmas snowflake muffins

## ingredients

*makes 12*

10 oz/280 g/2 cups all-purpose
   flour
1 tbsp baking powder
1 tsp ground allspice
pinch of salt
4 oz/115 g generous ½ cup
   dark brown sugar
2 eggs
3½ fl oz/100 ml/generous
   ⅓ cup milk
6 tbsp sunflower oil or 6 tbsp
   butter, melted and cooled
⅔ cup mixed dried fruit with
   cherries and nuts

### topping

1 lb/450 g ready-to-roll fondant
confectioners' sugar, for dusting
2½ tsp apricot jam
silver dragées, for decorating

## method

1 Line a 12-cup muffin pan with 12 muffin liners. Sift
   together the flour, baking powder, allspice, and salt into
   a large bowl. Stir in the brown sugar.

2 Place the eggs in a large pitcher or bowl and beat
   lightly, then beat in the milk and oil. Make a well in the
   center of the dry ingredients and pour in the liquid
   ingredients and dried fruit. Stir until combined; do not
   overmix. Spoon the batter into the muffin liners.

3 Bake in a preheated oven, 400°F/200°C, for 20 minutes,
   or until well risen, golden brown, and firm to the touch.
   Let cool in the pan for 5 minutes, then transfer to a wire
   rack and let cool completely.

4 Knead the fondant until pliable. Roll out the fondant
   on a surface dusted with confectioners' sugar to a
   thickness of ¼ inch/5 mm. Using a 2¾-inch/7-cm
   fluted cutter, cut out 12 "snowflakes."

5 Heat the apricot jam until runny, then brush over the
   tops of the muffins. Place a snowflake on top of each
   one, then decorate with silver dragées.

# brandied cherry muffins

## ingredients

*makes 12*

1 tbsp sunflower or peanut oil, for oiling (if using)
8 oz/225 g/generous 1½ cups all-purpose flour
1 tbsp baking powder
pinch of salt
1½ oz/45 g/3 tbsp butter
2 tbsp superfine sugar
1 large egg, beaten
7 fl oz/200 ml/scant 1 cup milk
2 tsp cherry brandy
10½ oz/300 g drained canned cherries, chopped

## method

1 Oil a 12-cup muffin pan with sunflower oil, or line it with 12 muffin liners.

2 Sift the flour, baking powder, and salt into a large mixing bowl.

3 In a separate large bowl, cream the butter and superfine sugar together, then stir in the beaten egg. Pour in the milk and cherry brandy, then add the chopped cherries and gently stir together. Add the cherry mixture to the flour mixture and then gently stir together until just combined. Do not overstir the batter—it is fine for it to be a little lumpy.

4 Divide the muffin batter among the 12 cups in the muffin pan or the muffin liners (each of the cups should be about two-thirds full). Transfer to a preheated oven, 400°F/200°C, and bake for 20–25 minutes until risen and golden. Remove from the oven and serve warm, or place them on a wire rack and let cool.

# apricot muffins with cointreau

## ingredients

*makes 12*

1 tbsp sunflower or peanut oil,
    for oiling (if using)
4½ oz/125 g/scant 1 cup
    self-rising flour
2 tsp baking powder
4½ oz/125 g/generous ½ cup
    butter
4½ oz/125 g/scant ⅔ cup
    superfine sugar
2 large eggs, beaten
4 fl oz/110 ml/½ cup milk
4 tbsp light cream
1 tbsp orange-flavored liqueur,
    such as Cointreau
3 oz/85 g/generous ½ cup no-soak
    dried apricots, chopped
3 oz/85 g/generous ½ cup no-soak
    dried dates, pitted and
    chopped

### topping

3 tbsp raw brown sugar
1 tsp ground cinnamon
1 tbsp freshly grated
    orange rind

## method

*1* Oil a 12-cup muffin pan with sunflower oil, or line it with 12 muffin liners.

*2* Sift the flour and baking powder together into a large mixing bowl.

*3* In a separate large bowl, cream together the butter and superfine sugar, then stir in the beaten eggs. Pour in the milk, cream, and orange-flavored liqueur, then add the chopped apricots and dates and gently mix together. Add the fruit mixture to the flour mixture and then gently stir together until just combined. Do not overstir the batter—it is fine for it to be a little lumpy.

*4* Divide the muffin batter evenly among the 12 cups in the muffin pan or the muffin liners (they should be about two-thirds full). To make the topping, place the raw sugar in a small bowl, then mix in the cinnamon and orange rind. Sprinkle the topping over the muffins, then transfer to the oven and bake in a preheated oven, 375°F/190°C, for 20 minutes, or until risen and golden. Remove the muffins from the oven and serve warm, or place them on a wire rack and let cool.

# vanilla hearts

## ingredients

*makes 12*

8 oz/225 g/1½ cups all-purpose flour, plus extra for dusting
8 oz/225 g/1 cup butter, cut into small pieces, plus extra for greasing
4½ oz/125 g/¾ cups superfine sugar, plus extra for dusting
1 tsp vanilla extract

## method

*1* Sift the flour into a large bowl. Add the butter and rub it in with your fingertips until the mixture resembles fine bread crumbs. Stir in the superfine sugar and vanilla extract and mix together to form a firm dough.

*2* Roll out the dough on a lightly floured counter to a thickness of 1 inch/2.5 cm. Stamp out 12 hearts with a heart-shaped cookie cutter measuring 2 inches/5 cm across and 1 inch/2.5 cm deep. Arrange the hearts on a lightly greased cookie sheet.

*3* Bake in a preheated oven, 350°F/180°C, for 15–20 minutes, or until the hearts are a light golden color. Transfer the vanilla hearts to a wire rack and let cool completely. Dust them with a little superfine sugar just before serving.

# simply
# delicious

# candy shop vanilla cupcakes

## ingredients

*makes 18*

5 oz/140 g/²/₃ cup butter, softened,
    or soft margarine
5 oz/140 g/³/₄ cup superfine sugar
1½ tsp vanilla extract
2 large eggs, lightly beaten
7 oz/200 g/scant 1½ cups
    self-rising flour

**topping**
8 oz/225 g/1 cup butter, softened
1 tbsp milk or cream
12 oz/350 g/3 cups
    confectioners' sugar
a selection of classic small
    candies, such as jelly beans,
    for decorating

## method

1 Put 18 paper baking cases into muffin pans, or place 18 double-layer paper cases on cookie sheets.

2 Place the butter and sugar in a large bowl and beat together until light and fluffy, then beat in the vanilla extract. Gradually beat in the eggs, then sift in the flour and fold into the mixture. Spoon the batter into the paper cases.

2 Bake in a preheated oven, 375°F/190°C, for 12–15 minutes, or until golden and springy to the touch. Transfer to a wire rack to cool completely.

3 To make the topping, place the butter and milk in a bowl and beat together. Gradually sift in the sugar and beat until smooth.

4 Place the buttercream in a pastry bag fitted with a small star tip and pipe the buttercream on top of each cake. Arrange the candies on top to decorate.

# drizzled honey cupcakes

## ingredients

*makes 12*

3 oz/85 g/generous ½ cup
    self-rising white flour
¼ tsp ground cinnamon
pinch of ground cloves
pinch of grated nutmeg
3 oz/85 g/6 tbsp butter, softened
3 oz/85 g/scant ½ cup
    superfine sugar
1 tbsp honey
finely grated rind of 1 orange
2 eggs, lightly beaten
1½ oz/40 g/¾ cup walnut
    pieces, minced

## topping

½ oz/15 g/⅛ cup walnut
    pieces, minced
¼ tsp ground cinnamon
2 tbsp honey
juice of 1 orange

## method

1 Put 12 paper baking cases in a muffin pan, or place 12 double-layer paper cases on a cookie sheet.

2 Sift the flour, cinnamon, cloves, and nutmeg together into a bowl. Put the butter and sugar in a separate bowl and beat together until light and fluffy. Beat in the honey and orange rind, then gradually add the eggs, beating well after each addition. Using a metal spoon, fold in the flour mixture. Stir in the walnuts, then spoon the batter into the paper cases.

3 Bake the cupcakes in a preheated oven, 375°F/190°C, for 20 minutes, or until well risen and golden brown. Transfer to a wire rack and let cool.

4 To make the topping, mix together the walnuts and cinnamon. Put the honey and orange juice in a pan and heat gently, stirring, until combined.

5 When the cupcakes have almost cooled, prick the tops all over with a fork or skewer and then drizzle with the warm honey mixture. Sprinkle the walnut mixture over the top of each cupcake and serve warm or cold.

# sticky gingerbread cupcakes

## ingredients

### makes 16

4 oz/115 g/generous ¾ cup
    all-purpose flour
2 tsp ground ginger
¾ tsp ground cinnamon
1 piece of preserved ginger,
    minced
¾ tsp baking soda
4 tbsp milk
3 oz/85 g/6 tbsp butter, softened,
    or soft margarine
2½ oz/70 g/generous ⅓ cup firmly
    packed brown sugar
2 tbsp molasses
2 eggs, lightly beaten
pieces of preserved ginger,
    to decorate

### topping

3 oz/85 g/6 tbsp butter, softened
6 oz/175 g/1½ cups
    confectioners' sugar
2 tbsp ginger syrup from the
    preserved ginger jar

## method

1 Put 16 paper baking cases in a muffin pan, or place 16 double-layer paper cases on cookie sheets.

2 Sift the flour, ground ginger, and cinnamon together into a bowl. Add the minced ginger and toss in the flour mixture until well coated. In a separate bowl, dissolve the baking soda in the milk.

3 Put the butter and sugar in a bowl and beat together until fluffy. Beat in the molasses, then gradually add the eggs, beating well after each addition. Beat in the flour mixture, then gradually beat in the milk. Spoon the batter into the paper cases.

4 Bake in a preheated oven, 325°F/160°C, for 20 minutes, or until well risen and golden brown. Transfer to a wire rack and let cool.

5 To make the frosting, put the butter in a bowl and beat until fluffy. Sift in the sugar, add the ginger syrup, and beat together until smooth and creamy. Slice the preserved ginger into thin slivers or chop finely.

6 When the cupcakes are cold, spread a little frosting over each of the cupcakes, then decorate with pieces of ginger.

# marbled chocolate cupcakes

## ingredients

*makes 21*

6 oz/175 g/¾ cup soft margarine
6 oz/175 g/generous ¾ cup
    superfine sugar
3 eggs
6 oz/175 g/scant 1¼ cups
    self-rising white flour
2 tbsp milk
2 oz/55 g semisweet chocolate,
    melted

## method

1 Put 21 paper baking cases in muffin pans, or place 21 double-layer paper cases on cookie sheets.

2 Put the margarine, sugar, eggs, flour, and milk in a large bowl and, using an electric hand whisk, beat together until just smooth.

3 Divide the batter between 2 bowls. Add the melted chocolate to one bowl and stir together until well mixed. Using a teaspoon, and alternating the chocolate batter with the plain batter, put four half-teaspoons into each paper case.

4 Bake in a preheated oven, 350°F/180°C, for 20 minutes, or until well risen and springy to the touch. Transfer to a wire rack and let cool.

## variation

Add the grated rind and juice of ½ small orange and a few drops of orange food coloring to the plain cake mixture.

# carrot cake

## ingredients

*makes 6*

butter, for greasing
4 oz/115 g/scant 1 cup
    self-rising flour
pinch of salt
1 tsp ground allspice
$\frac{1}{2}$ tsp ground nutmeg
6 oz/175 g/$\frac{3}{4}$ cup soft
    brown sugar
2 eggs, beaten
5 tbsp sunflower oil
6 oz/175 g/$\frac{3}{4}$ cup (packed)
    grated carrots
1 banana, chopped
1 oz/25 g/$\frac{1}{4}$ cup chopped
    toasted mixed nuts

### topping

1$\frac{1}{2}$ oz/45 g/3 tbsp butter, softened
3 tbsp cream cheese
6 oz/175 g/1$\frac{1}{2}$ cups
    confectioners' sugar, sifted
1 tsp orange juice
grated rind of $\frac{1}{2}$ orange
walnut halves or pieces,
    to decorate

## method

1 Grease a 7-inch/18-cm square cake pan with butter and line with parchment paper. Sift the flour, salt, allspice, and nutmeg into a bowl. Stir in the brown sugar, then stir in the eggs and oil. Add the carrots, banana, and chopped mixed nuts and mix together well.

2 Spoon the mixture into the prepared cake pan and level the surface. Transfer to a preheated oven, 375°F/190°C, and bake for 55 minutes, or until golden and just firm to the touch. Remove from the oven and let cool. When cool enough to handle, turn out on to a wire rack and let cool completely.

3 To make the frosting, put the butter, cream cheese, confectioners' sugar, and orange juice and rind into a bowl and beat together until creamy. Spread the frosting over the top of the cold cake, then use a fork to make shallow wavy lines in the frosting. Scatter over the walnuts, cut the cake into bars, and serve.

# queen cakes

## ingredients

*makes 18*

4 oz/115 g/½ cup butter, softened, or soft margarine
4 oz/115 g/generous ½ cup superfine sugar
2 large eggs, lightly beaten
4 tsp lemon juice
6 oz/175 g/scant 1¼ cups self-rising white flour
4 oz/115 g/¾ cup currants
2–4 tbsp milk, if necessary

## method

*1* Put 18 muffin liners in muffin pans.

*2* Put the butter and sugar in a bowl and beat together until light and fluffy. Gradually beat in the eggs, then beat in the lemon juice with 1 tablespoon of the flour. Using a metal spoon, fold in the remaining flour and the currants, adding a little milk if necessary to give a soft dropping consistency. Spoon the batter into the muffin liners.

*3* Bake the cupcakes in a preheated oven, 375°F/190°C, for 15–20 minutes, or until well risen and golden brown. Transfer to a wire rack and let cool.

# donut muffins

## ingredients

*makes 12*

6 oz/175 g/¾ cup butter, softened,
    plus extra for greasing
7 oz/200 g/1 cup
    superfine sugar
2 large eggs, lightly beaten
13 oz/375 g/generous
    2½ cups all-purpose flour
¾ tbsp baking powder
¼ tsp baking soda
pinch of salt
½ tsp freshly grated nutmeg
9 fl oz/250 ml/generous
    1 cup milk

### topping

3½ oz/100 g/½ cup superfine sugar
1 tsp ground cinnamon
2 tbsp butter, melted

## method

1 Grease a deep 12-cup muffin pan. In a large bowl, beat
the butter and sugar together until light and creamy.
Add the eggs, a little at a time, beating well between
additions.

2 Sift the flour, baking powder, baking soda, salt, and
nutmeg together. Add half to the creamed mixture
with half of the milk. Gently fold the ingredients
together before incorporating the remaining flour
and milk. Spoon the mixture into the prepared muffin
pan, filling each pan to about two-thirds full. Bake
in a preheated oven, 350°F/180°C, for 15–20 minutes,
or until the muffins are lightly brown and firm to
the touch.

3 For the topping, mix the sugar and cinnamon together.
While the muffins are still warm from the oven, brush
lightly with melted butter, and sprinkle over the
cinnamon and sugar mixture. Eat warm or cold.

# lime & poppy seed muffins

## ingredients

*makes 12*

6 fl oz/175 ml/¾ cup sunflower or peanut oil, plus extra for oiling (if using)

8 oz/225 g/1½ cups all-purpose flour

1 tsp baking powder

½ tsp salt

8 oz/225 g/scant 1¼ cups superfine sugar

1 large egg

1 large egg white

5 fl oz/150 ml/⅔ cup milk

1 tbsp lime juice

1 tbsp grated lime rind

2 tsp poppy seeds

### decoration

2 tsp grated lime rind

1–2 tsp poppy seeds

## method

1 Oil a 12-cup muffin pan with sunflower oil, or line it with 12 muffin liners.

2 Sift the flour, baking powder, and salt into a mixing bowl. Then add the superfine sugar and stir together.

3 In a separate bowl, whisk the egg, egg white, remaining sunflower oil, and milk together, then stir in the lime juice and grated lime rind. Add the egg mixture to the flour mixture, then add the poppy seeds and gently stir together. Do not overstir the batter—it is fine for it to be a little lumpy.

4 Divide the muffin batter evenly among the 12 cups in the muffin pan or the muffin liners (they should be about two-thirds full). Sprinkle over the grated lime rind and poppy seeds to decorate, then bake in a preheated oven, 375°F/190°C, for 25 minutes, or until risen and golden. Serve the muffins warm, or place them on a wire rack and let cool.

# buttermilk scones

## ingredients

### makes 8

10½ oz/300 g/generous
   2 cups self-rising flour,
   plus extra for dusting
1 tsp baking powder
pinch of salt
2 oz/60 g/4 tbsp cold butter,
   cut into pieces, plus extra
   for greasing
1½ oz/40 g/scant ¼ cup golden
   superfine sugar
10 fl oz/300 ml/1¼ cups buttermilk
2 tbsp milk
whipped cream, to serve
strawberry jelly, to serve

## method

1 Sift the flour, baking powder, and salt into a bowl. Add the butter and rub in until the mixture resembles fine bread crumbs. Add the sugar and buttermilk and quickly mix together.

2 Turn the mixture out onto a floured counter and knead lightly. Roll out to 1-inch/2.5-cm thick. Using a 2½-inch/6-cm plain or fluted cutter, stamp out biscuits and place on a greased cookie sheet. Gather the trimmings, re-roll, and stamp out more biscuits until all the dough is used up.

3 Brush the tops of the biscuits with milk. Bake in a preheated oven, 425°F/220°C, for 12–15 minutes, or until well risen and golden. Transfer to a wire rack to cool. Split and serve with whipped cream and strawberry jelly.

# petticoat tail shortbread

## ingredients

*makes 8*

6 oz/175 g/scant 1¼ cups
    all-purpose flour, plus
    1 tbsp for dusting
pinch of salt
2 oz /55 g/generous ¼ cup
    superfine sugar
4 oz/115 g/½ cup butter, cut
    into small pieces, plus extra
    for greasing
2 tsp golden superfine sugar

## method

1 Mix together the flour, salt, and sugar. Rub the butter into the dry ingredients. Continue to work the mixture until it forms a soft dough. Make sure you do not overwork the dough or the shortbread will be tough, not crumbly as it should be.

2 Lightly press the dough into a greased 20-cm/8-inch fluted cake pan. Alternatively, roll out the dough on a lightly floured counter, place on a cookie sheet, and pinch the edges to form a scalloped pattern.

3 Mark into 8 pieces with a knife. Prick the shortbread all over with a fork and bake in the center of a preheated oven, 300°F/150°C, for 45–50 minutes until the shortbread is firm and just colored.

4 Let cool in the tin and dredge with the sugar. Cut into portions and remove to a wire rack. Store in an airtight container in a cool place until needed.

# rock drops

## ingredients

*makes 8*

3 oz/100 g/scant ½ cup butter,
    cut into small pieces, plus
    extra for greasing
7 oz/200 g/1½ cups
    all-purpose flour
2 tsp baking powder
2¾ oz/75 g/scant ½ cup golden
    superfine sugar
3½ oz/100 g/½ cup golden raisins
1 oz/25 g/¼ cup candied cherries,
    finely chopped
1 egg, beaten
2 tbsp milk

## method

1 Lightly grease a cookie sheet, large enough for 8 big
    rock drops, with a little butter.

2 Sift the flour and baking powder into a mixing bowl.
    Rub in the butter with your fingertips until the mixture
    resembles fine bread crumbs. Stir in the sugar, golden
    raisins, and chopped candied cherries, mixing well.
    Add the beaten egg and the milk to the mixture and
    mix to form a soft dough.

3 Spoon 8 mounds of the mixture onto the prepared
    cookie sheet, spacing them well apart as they will
    spread while cooking. Bake in a preheated oven,
    400°F/200°C, for 15–20 minutes, until firm to the touch.

4 Remove the rock drops from the cookie sheet. Either
    serve immediately or transfer to a wire rack and let cool
    before serving.

# healthy options

# banana muffins with cinnamon frosting

## ingredients

*makes 12*

5½ oz/150 g/generous
    1 cup gluten-free
    all-purpose flour
1 tsp gluten-free baking powder
pinch of salt
5½ oz/150 g/generous ¾ cup
    superfine sugar
6 tbsp dairy-free milk
2 eggs, lightly beaten
5½ oz/150 g/⅔ cup dairy-free
    margarine, melted
2 small bananas, mashed

### frosting

1¾ oz/50 g/scant ¼ cup vegan
    cream cheese
2 tbsp dairy-free margarine
¼ tsp ground cinnamon
3¼ oz/90 g/scant 1 cup
    confectioners' sugar

## method

1 Place 12 large muffin liners in a deep muffin pan. Sift the flour, baking powder, and salt together into a mixing bowl. Stir in the sugar.

2 Whisk the milk, eggs, and margarine together in a separate bowl until combined. Slowly stir into the flour mixture without beating. Fold in the mashed bananas.

3 Spoon the mixture into the muffin liners and bake in a preheated oven, 400°F/200°C, for 20 minutes until risen and golden. Turn out onto a wire rack and let cool.

4 To make the frosting, beat the cream cheese and margarine together in a bowl, then beat in the cinnamon and confectioners' sugar until smooth and creamy. Chill the frosting in the refrigerator for about 15 minutes to firm up, then top each muffin with a spoonful.

# banana & date muffins

## ingredients

*makes 12*

vegetable oil cooking spray,
    for oiling (if using)
8 oz/225 g/1½ cups
    all-purpose flour
2 tsp baking powder
¼ tsp salt
½ tsp allspice
5 tbsp superfine sugar
2 large egg whites
2 ripe bananas, sliced
2 oz/55 g/scant ½ cup no-soak
    dried dates, pitted and
    chopped
4 tbsp skim milk
5 tbsp maple syrup

## method

*1* Spray a 12-cup muffin pan with vegetable oil cooking spray, or line it with 12 muffin liners. Sift the flour, baking powder, salt, and allspice into a mixing bowl. Add the superfine sugar and mix together.

*2* In a separate bowl, whisk the egg whites together. Mash the sliced bananas in a separate bowl, then add them to the egg whites. Add the dates, then pour in the skim milk and maple syrup and stir together gently to mix. Add the banana and date mixture to the flour mixture and then gently stir together until just combined. Do not overstir the batter—it is fine for it to be a little lumpy.

*3* Divide the muffin batter evenly among the 12 cups in the muffin pan or the muffin liners (they should be about two-thirds full). Bake in a preheated oven, 400°F/200°C, for 25 minutes, or until risen and golden. Remove the muffins from the oven and serve warm, or place them on a wire rack and let cool.

# wheat germ, banana & pumpkin seed muffins

## ingredients

### makes 12

6 tbsp sunflower oil, plus extra for greasing

5 oz/140 g/1 cup all-purpose flour

1 tbsp baking powder

4 oz/115 g/generous ½ cup superfine sugar

5 oz/140 g/1¼ cups wheat germ

3 oz/85 g/⅓ cup pumpkin seeds

2 bananas

5 fl oz/150 ml/about ⅔ cup skim milk

2 eggs

## method

*1* Grease a 12-cup muffin pan. Sift together the flour and baking powder into a large bowl. Stir in the sugar, wheat germ, and ¼ cup of the pumpkin seeds. Mash the bananas and place in a pitcher, then add enough milk to make up the puree to a heaping 1 cup.

*2* Place the eggs in a large pitcher or bowl and beat lightly, then beat in the banana and milk mixture and the oil. Make a well in the center of the dry ingredients and pour in the beaten liquid ingredients. Stir gently until just combined; do not overmix. Spoon the batter into the muffin pan. Sprinkle the remaining pumpkin seeds over the top.

*3* Bake in a preheated oven, 400°F/200°C, for 20 minutes, or until well risen, golden brown, and firm to the touch. Let cool in the pan for 5 minutes, then serve warm or transfer to a wire rack to cool completely.

# muesli muffins

## ingredients

### makes 12

5 oz/140 g/1 cup all-purpose flour

1 tbsp baking powder

10 oz/280 g/generous 1¾ cups
  unsweetened muesli

4 oz/115 g/generous ½ cup light
  brown sugar

2 eggs

9 fl oz/250 ml/generous 1 cup
  buttermilk

6 tbsp sunflower oil

## method

1  Line a 12-cup muffin pan with 12 muffin liners. Sift together the flour and baking powder into a large bowl. Stir in the muesli and sugar.

2  Place the eggs in a large pitcher or bowl and beat lightly, then beat in the buttermilk and oil. Make a well in the center of the dry ingredients and pour in the beaten liquid ingredients. Stir gently until just combined; do not overmix. Spoon the batter into the muffin liners.

3  Bake in a preheated oven, 400°F/200°C, for 20 minutes, or until well risen, golden brown, and firm to the touch. Let cool in the pan for 5 minutes, then serve warm or transfer to a wire rack to cool completely.

# yogurt & spice muffins

## ingredients

*makes 12*

5 oz/140 g/1 cup whole wheat
   flour
5 oz/140 g/1 cup all-purpose flour
1 tbsp baking powder
½ tsp baking soda
4 tsp apple pie spice
4 oz/115 g/generous ½ cup
   superfine sugar
3½ oz/100 g/½ cup mixed
   dried fruit
2 eggs
9 fl oz/250 ml/generous 1 cup
   low-fat plain yogurt
6 tbsp sunflower oil

## method

*1* Place 12 large muffin liners in a deep muffin pan. Sift together both types of flour, the baking powder, baking soda, and apple pie spice into a large bowl, adding any bran left in the strainer. Stir in the sugar and dried fruit.

*2* Place the eggs in a large pitcher or bowl and beat lightly, then beat in the yogurt and oil. Make a well in the center of the dry ingredients and pour in the beaten liquid ingredients. Stir gently until just combined; do not overmix. Spoon the batter into the muffin liners.

*3* Bake in a preheated oven, 400°F/200°C, for 20 minutes, or until well risen, golden brown, and firm to the touch. Let cool in the pan for 5 minutes, then serve warm or transfer to a wire rack to cool completely.

# three grain muffins

## ingredients

*makes 12*

6 tbsp sunflower oil, plus extra
  for greasing
2¾ oz/75 g/½ cup whole wheat
  flour
2¾ oz/75 g/½ cup all-purpose flour
1 tbsp baking powder
4 oz/115 g/generous ½ cup dark
  brown sugar
2¼ oz/60 g/scant ½ cup medium
  cornmeal
2½ oz/70 g/scant 1 cup rolled oats
2 eggs
9 fl oz/250 ml/generous 1 cup
  buttermilk
1 tsp vanilla extract

## method

1 Grease a 12-cup muffin pan. Sift together the flours and the baking powder into a large bowl, adding any bran left in the strainer. Stir in the sugar, cornmeal, and oats.

2 Place the eggs in a large pitcher or bowl and beat lightly, then beat in the buttermilk, oil, and vanilla extract. Make a well in the center of the dry ingredients and pour in the beaten liquid ingredients. Stir gently until just combined; do not overmix. Spoon the batter into the muffin pan.

3 Bake in a preheated oven, 400°F/200°C, for 20 minutes, or until well risen, golden brown, and firm to the touch. Let cool in the pan for 5 minutes, then serve warm or transfer to a wire rack to cool completely.

# apple & raspberry muffins

## ingredients

*makes 12*

3 large baking apples,
    peeled and cored
16 fl oz/450 ml/generous
    1½ cups water
1½ tsp allspice
vegetable oil cooking spray,
    for oiling (if using)
10½ oz/300 g/generous
    2 cups all-purpose
    whole wheat flour
1 tbsp baking powder
¼ tsp salt
3 tbsp superfine sugar
3 oz/85 g/generous 1 cup
    fresh raspberries

## method

1 Thinly slice 2 baking apples and place them in a pan with 6 tablespoons of the water. Bring to a boil, then reduce the heat. Stir in ½ teaspoon of the allspice, cover the pan, and let simmer, stirring occasionally, for 15–20 minutes until the water has been absorbed. Remove from the heat and let cool. Blend in a food processor until smooth. Stir in the remaining water and mix well.

2 Spray a 12-cup muffin pan with vegetable oil cooking spray, or line it with 12 muffin liners. Sift the flour, baking powder, salt, and remaining allspice into a mixing bowl. Then stir in the sugar.

3 Chop the remaining apple and add to the flour mixture. Add the raspberries, then combine gently with the flour mixture until lightly coated. Finally, gently stir in the cooled apple/water mixture. Do not overstir the batter—it is fine for it to be a little lumpy.

4 Divide the muffin batter evenly among the 12 cups in the muffin pan or the muffin liners (they should be about two-thirds full). Bake in a preheated oven, 400°F/200°C, for 25 minutes, or until risen and golden. Remove the muffins from the oven and serve warm, or place them on a wire rack and let cool.

# dairy-free berry muffins

## ingredients

*makes 12*

1 large baking apple, peeled, cored, and thinly sliced
3 tbsp water
1 tsp allspice
2 tbsp sunflower or peanut oil, plus extra for oiling (if using)
8 oz/225 g/1½ cups all-purpose white or whole wheat flour
1 tbsp baking powder
¼ tsp salt
1½ oz/40 g/scant ½ cup wheat germ
1 oz/25 g/¼ cup fresh raspberries
1 oz/25 g/¼ cup fresh strawberries, hulled and chopped
6 tbsp maple syrup
6 fl oz/175 ml/¾ cup apple juice

## method

1 Place the sliced apple and the water in a pan and bring to a boil. Reduce the heat and stir in half of the allspice, then cover the pan and let simmer, stirring occasionally, for 15–20 minutes, or until the water has been absorbed. Remove the pan from the heat and let cool. Transfer the apple mixture to a food processor and blend until smooth.

2 Lightly oil a 12-cup muffin pan with a little sunflower oil, or line the pan with 12 muffin liners. Sift the flour, baking powder, salt, and the remaining allspice into a mixing bowl, then stir in the wheat germ.

3 In a separate bowl, mix the raspberries, chopped strawberries, maple syrup, remaining oil, puréed apple, and apple juice together. Add the fruit mixture to the flour mixture and gently stir together until just combined. Do not overstir the batter—it is fine for it to be a little lumpy.

4 Divide the muffin batter evenly among the 12 cups in the muffin pan or the muffin liners (they should be about two-thirds full). Transfer to a preheated oven, 375°F/190°C, and bake for 25 minutes, or until risen and golden. Remove from the oven and serve warm, or place them on a wire rack and let cool.

# fruity muffins

## ingredients

*makes 10*

10 oz/275 g/2 cups self-rising
    whole wheat flour
2 tsp baking powder
2 tbsp brown sugar
3 oz/85 g/generous ½ cup no-soak
    dried apricots, finely chopped
1 banana, mashed with
    1 tbsp orange juice
1 tsp finely grated orange rind
10 fl oz/300 ml/1¼ cups skim milk
1 large egg, beaten
3 tbsp sunflower or peanut oil
2 tbsp rolled oats
fruit spread, honey, or maple syrup,
    to serve

## method

*1* Line a 12-cup muffin pan with 10 muffin liners. Sift the
flour and baking powder into a mixing bowl, adding
any bran that remain in the strainer. Stir in the sugar
and chopped apricots.

*2* Make a well in the center and add the mashed banana,
orange rind, milk, beaten egg, and oil. Mix together
well to form a thick batter and divide the mixture
evenly among the muffin liners.

*3* Sprinkle with a few rolled oats and bake in a preheated
oven, 400°F/200°C, for 25–30 minutes until well risen
and firm to the touch, or until a toothpick inserted into
the center comes out clean.

*4* Remove the muffins from the oven and place them
on a wire rack to cool slightly. Serve the muffins
while still warm with a little fruit spread, honey,
or maple syrup.

# cranberry muffins

## ingredients

*makes 10*

6 oz/175 g/scant 1¼ cups
self-rising white flour

2 oz/55 g/scant ½ cup self-rising
whole wheat flour

1 tsp ground cinnamon

½ tsp baking soda

1 egg, beaten

2½ oz/70 g/scant ¼ cup thin-cut
orange marmalade

5 fl oz/150 ml/⅔ cup
1 or 2 percent milk

5 tbsp corn oil

4 oz/115 g peeled, cored, and
finely diced eating apple

4 oz/115 g/⅔ cup fresh or frozen
cranberries, thawed if frozen

1 tbsp rolled oats

freshly squeezed orange juice,
to serve

## method

1 Place 10 large muffin liners in a deep muffin pan. Put the two flours, cinnamon, and baking soda into a mixing bowl and combine thoroughly.

2 Make a well in the center of the flour mixture. In a separate bowl, blend the egg with the marmalade until well combined. Beat the milk and oil into the egg mixture, then pour into the dry ingredients, stirring lightly. Do not overmix—the batter should be slightly lumpy. Quickly stir in the apple and cranberries.

3 Spoon the batter evenly into the muffin liners and sprinkle the oats over each muffin. Bake in a preheated oven, 400°F/200°C, for 20–25 minutes, or until well risen and golden, and a skewer inserted into the center of a muffin comes out clean.

4 Lift out the muffins and transfer onto a wire rack. Let stand for 5–10 minutes, or until slightly cooled. Peel off the muffin cases and serve warm with glasses of freshly squeezed orange juice. These muffins are best eaten on the day they are made—any leftover muffins should be stored in an airtight container and consumed within 24 hours.

# blueberry muffins

## ingredients

### *makes 12*

vegetable oil cooking spray,
      for oiling (if using)
8 oz/225 g/generous
      1½ cups all-purpose flour
1 tsp baking soda
¼ tsp salt
1 tsp allspice
4 oz/115 g/generous ½ cup
      superfine sugar
3 large egg whites
1½ oz/45 g/3 tbsp lowfat
      margarine
5 fl oz/150 ml/⅔ cup thick
      lowfat plain or blueberry-
      flavored yogurt
1 tsp vanilla extract
3 oz/85 g/¾ cup
      fresh blueberries

## method

*1* Spray a 12-cup muffin pan with vegetable oil cooking spray, or line it with 12 muffin liners.

*2* Sift the flour, baking soda, salt, and half of the allspice into a large mixing bowl. Add 6 tablespoons of the superfine sugar and mix together.

*3* In a separate bowl, whisk the egg whites together. Add the margarine, yogurt, and vanilla extract and mix together well, then stir in the fresh blueberries until thoroughly mixed. Add the fruit mixture to the flour mixture, then gently stir together until just combined. Do not overstir the batter—it is fine for it to be a little lumpy.

*4* Divide the muffin batter evenly among the 12 cups in the muffin pan or the muffin liners (they should be about two-thirds full). Mix the remaining sugar with the remaining allspice, then sprinkle the mixture over the muffins. Transfer to a preheated oven, 375°F/190°C, and bake for 25 minutes, or until risen and golden. Remove the muffins from the oven and serve warm, or place them on a wire rack and let cool.

# honey & lemon muffins

## ingredients

*makes 12*

1¾ oz/50 g/¼ cup unrefined
   superfine sugar
1 oz/30 g/2 tbsp unsalted butter,
   melted and cooled slightly
5 fl oz/150 ml/⅔ cup buttermilk
2 eggs, beaten
4 tbsp flower honey
finely grated rind of 1 lemon
   and juice of ½ lemon
8 oz/225 g/generous 1½ cups
   all-purpose flour
5½ oz/150 g/2¾ cups oat bran
1½ tbsp baking powder

## method

1 Line a 12-cup muffin pan with muffin liners. Put the
   sugar into a pitcher and add the butter, buttermilk,
   eggs, half the honey, and lemon rind. Mix briefly
   to combine.

2 Sift the flour into a large mixing bowl, add the oat bran
   and baking powder, and stir to combine. Make a well in
   the center of the flour mixture and add the buttermilk
   mixture. Quickly mix together—do not overmix; the
   batter should be slightly lumpy.

3 Spoon the batter into the muffin liners and bake in a
   preheated oven, 350°F/180°C, for 25 minutes. Turn out
   onto a wire rack.

4 Mix the lemon juice with the remaining honey in a
   small bowl or pitcher and drizzle over the muffins
   while they are still hot. Let the muffins stand for
   10 minutes before serving.

# moist orange & almond muffins

## ingredients

*makes 12*

2 oranges
3 1/2 fl oz/100 ml/ about 1/3 cup milk
1 2/3 cups all-purpose flour
1 tbsp baking powder
pinch of salt
generous 1/2 cup superfine sugar
2/3 cup ground almonds
2 eggs
6 tbsp sunflower oil or 6 tbsp
    butter, melted and cooled
1/2 tsp almond extract
1 1/2 oz/40 g/scant 1/4 cup raw
    brown sugar

## method

1 Line a 12-cup muffin pan with muffin liners. Finely grate the rind from the oranges and squeeze the juice. Add enough milk to make the juice up to a generous 1 cup, then stir in the orange rind. Sift together the flour, baking powder, and salt into a large bowl. Stir in the superfine sugar and ground almonds.

2 Place the eggs in a bowl and beat lightly, then beat in the orange mixture, oil, and almond extract. Make a well in the center of the dry ingredients, pour in the liquid ingredients, and mix. Spoon the batter into the muffin liners. Sprinkle the raw brown sugar over the tops.

3 Bake in a preheated oven, 400°F/200°C, for 20 minutes, or until well risen, golden brown, and firm to the touch. Let cool in the pan for 5 minutes, then serve warm or transfer to a wire rack to cool completely.

# spiced carrot cake muffins

## ingredients

### makes 12

2 tbsp sunflower or peanut oil, plus
    extra for oiling (if using)
scant ¾ cup all-purpose white flour
3½ oz/100 g/¾ cup all-purpose
    whole wheat flour
1 tsp baking soda
¼ tsp salt
1 tsp ground cinnamon
½ tsp ground ginger
2 tbsp superfine sugar
2 large egg whites
5 tbsp skim or lowfat milk
8 oz/225 g canned pineapple
    chunks in juice, drained,
    chopped, and mashed
9 oz/250 g carrots, grated
1½ oz/40 g/¼ cup golden raisins
1½ oz/40 g/scant ½ cup shelled
    walnuts, chopped

### topping

8 oz/225 g/1⅛ cups lowfat
    soft cheese
1⅓ tbsp superfine sugar
1½ tsp vanilla extract
1½ tsp ground cinnamon

## method

1 Oil a 12-cup muffin pan with sunflower oil, or line it with 12 muffin liners. Sift both flours, baking soda, salt, cinnamon, and ginger into a mixing bowl. Add the superfine sugar and mix together.

2 In a separate bowl, whisk the egg whites together, then mix in the milk and remaining oil. Add the mashed pineapple, the carrots, golden raisins, and walnuts and stir together gently. Add the fruit mixture to the flour mixture and gently stir until just combined. Do not overstir the batter—it is fine for it to be a little lumpy.

3 Divide the muffin batter evenly between the 12 cups in the muffin pan or the muffin liners (they should be about two-thirds full). Transfer to a preheated oven, 375°F/190°C, and bake for 25 minutes, or until risen and golden, then let cool on a wire rack.

4 While the muffins are in the oven, make the topping. Place the soft cheese in a mixing bowl with the superfine sugar, vanilla extract, and 1 teaspoon of the cinnamon. Mix together well, then cover with plastic wrap and transfer to the refrigerator until ready to use.

5 When the muffins have cooled to room temperature, remove the topping from the refrigerator and spread some evenly over the top of each muffin. Lightly sprinkle over the remaining cinnamon and serve.

# spiced whole wheat muffins

## ingredients

*serves 6*

canola or vegetable oil spray
4½ oz/125 g/scant 1 cup
    all-purpose flour
½ tsp baking powder
2 oz/55 g/scant ½ cup
    whole wheat flour
½ tsp ground allspice
1 tbsp canola or vegetable oil
1 egg, lightly beaten
5 fl oz/150 ml/⅔ cup buttermilk
1 tsp grated orange zest
1 tbsp freshly squeezed orange
    juice
1 tsp low-sugar marmalade,
    for glazing

### filling

3½ oz/100 g/generous ⅓ cup
    0% fat strained plain yogurt
1 tsp low-sugar marmalade
½ tsp grated orange zest
3½ oz/100 g/scant ½ cup fresh
    raspberries

## method

**1** Spray a 6-cup muffin pan lightly with oil. Sift the all-purpose flour with the baking powder into a large mixing bowl. Using a fork, stir in the whole wheat flour and allspice until thoroughly mixed. Pour in the oil and rub into the flour mixture with your fingertips.

**2** In a separate bowl, mix the egg, buttermilk, and orange zest and juice together, then pour into the center of the flour mixture and mix with a metal spoon, being careful not to overmix—the batter should look a little uneven and lumpy.

**3** Spoon the batter into the prepared pan to come about three-quarters of the way up the sides of each cup. Bake in a preheated oven, 325°F/160°C, for 30 minutes, or until golden brown and a skewer inserted into the center of a muffin comes out clean. Remove from the oven and transfer to a wire rack. Brush with the marmalade and let cool.

**4** For the filling, mix the yogurt with the marmalade and orange zest. Cut the warm muffins through the center and fill with the yogurt mixture and raspberries.

# high-energy muffins

## ingredients

*makes 12*

5 tbsp sunflower or peanut oil,
  plus extra for oiling (if using)
3 oz/85 g/generous ½ cup
  whole wheat flour
1¾ oz/50 g/1½ cup quick-cooking
  oats
1½ oz/40 g/scant ½ cup
  wheat germ
2 tsp baking powder
1 tsp ground cinnamon
¼ tsp salt
1½ oz/40 g/⅓ cup
  no-soak dried dates,
  pitted and chopped
2 oz/55 g/⅓ cup
  golden raisins
4 oz/115 g/3½ cups
  bran flakes
7 fl oz/200 ml/scant 1 cup milk
2 large eggs, beaten
5 tbsp honey
4 tbsp corn syrup
4 tbsp molasses

## method

1 Oil a 12-cup muffin pan with sunflower oil, or line it with 12 muffin liners. Place the flour, oats, wheat germ, baking powder, cinnamon, and salt in a mixing bowl and mix together.

2 In a separate bowl, mix the dates, golden raisins, and bran flakes together. Pour in the milk and stir together. Then stir in the beaten eggs, honey, corn syrup, molasses, and remaining oil. Add the fruit mixture to the flour mixture and then gently stir together until just combined. Do not overstir the batter—it is fine for it to be a little lumpy.

3 Divide the muffin batter evenly among the 12 cups in the muffin pan or the muffin liners (they should be about two-thirds full). Transfer to a preheated oven, 375°F/190°C, and bake for 20–25 minutes until risen and golden. Remove the muffins from the oven and serve warm, or place them on a wire rack and let cool.

# sugarless chocolate muffins

## ingredients

*makes 12*

4 tbsp sunflower or peanut oil,
    plus extra for oiling (if using)
8 oz/225 g/generous 1½ cups
    all-purpose flour
1 tbsp baking powder
1 tbsp unsweetened cocoa
½ tsp allspice
2 large eggs
6 fl oz/175 ml/¾ cup unsweetened
    orange juice
1 tsp grated orange rind
1½ oz/40 g/generous ½ cup fresh
    blueberries

## method

*1* Oil a 12-cup muffin pan with sunflower oil, or line it
    with 12 muffin liners. Sift the flour, baking powder,
    cocoa, and allspice into a large mixing bowl.

*2* In a separate bowl, whisk the eggs and the remaining
    sunflower oil together. Pour in the orange juice, add
    the grated orange rind and the blueberries, and stir
    together gently to mix. Add the egg and fruit mixture
    to the flour mixture and then gently stir together until
    just combined. Do not overstir the batter—it is fine for
    it to be a little lumpy.

*3* Divide the muffin batter evenly among the 12 cups
    in the muffin pan or the muffin liners (they should be
    about two-thirds full). Transfer to a preheated oven,
    400°F/200°C, and bake for 20 minutes, or until risen and
    golden. Serve the muffins warm, or place them
    on a wire rack and let cool.

# index